A Slant of Wind

Jenvery 10, 2021
To Leurg fellw euthers
heren ir our life!

Best wishes always

A Slant of Wind

A Summer Afternoon's Reflections on Writing and Publishing

Arthur T. Vanderbilt II

SERVING
HOUSE
BOOKS

A Slant of Wind:

A Summer Afternoon's Reflections on Writing and Publishing

Copyright © Arthur T. Vanderbilt II

Published by Serving House Books

Copenhagen, Denmark, and South Orange, NJ

www.servinghousebooks.com

ISBN: 978-1-947175-48-8

Library of Congress Control Number: 2020952069

Member of The Independent Book Publishers Association

First Serving House Books Edition 2021

Cover Photograph: Walter Cummins

Author Photograph: Hayley Croft

Serving House Books Logo: Barry Lereng Wilmont

Our minds and souls contain volumes inscribed by our experiences and emotions; each individual's consciousness is a collection of memories we've cataloged and stored inside us, a private library of a life lived. It is something that no one else can entirely share, one that burns down and disappears when we die. But if you can take something from that internal collection and share it--with one person or with the larger world, on the page or in a story recited — it takes on a life of its own.

— Susan Orlean from *The Library Book*

To Walter Cummins:
friend, fellow author and Florham explorer

Books by Arthur T. Vanderbilt II

Changing Law: A Biography of Arthur T. Vanderbilt

An Introduction to the Study of Law

Jersey Justice: Three Hundred Years of the New Jersey Judiciary

Law School: Briefing for a Legal Education

Treasure Wreck: The Fortunes and Fate of the Pirate Ship Whydah

Fortune's Children: The Fall of the House of Vanderbilt

Golden Days: Memories of a Golden Retriever

New Jersey's Judicial Revolution: A Political Miracle

The Making of a Bestseller: From Author to Reader

Jersey Jurists: Profiles in the Law

Gardening in Eden: The Joys of Planning and Tending a Garden

Best-Kept Boy in the World: The Short Scandalous Life of Denham Fouts

Florham: An American Treasure. (co-author)

The Richest and Most Famous Private Chef in the World: Joseph Donon. (co-author)

The Soul of a House: Adventures in Building an Antique Retirement Account

Olmsted's Vision: The Landscape of Florham. (co-author)

Remaking Florham: From Gilded Age Estate to Campus of Fairleigh Dickinson University (co-author).

CONTENTS

PREFACE

"SUMMER AFTERNOON," MUSED HENRY JAMES, "summer afternoon; to me those have always been the most beautiful words in the English language."
Sitting under the old oaks on a drowsy summer afternoon, as insects drone overhead and thoughts drift like shadows on the lawn, I think back over — can it be? — fifty years of writing books.

Whenever I pass the bookcase in my study packed with my books, it always amazes me: how did so many accumulate over five decades? When did that happen? Hardcovers. Paperbacks. Book Club editions. Condensed editions. Anthologies. Foreign editions. Large print editions. Audio books. Reprints. The wooden file boxes jammed with magazines, journals, newspapers containing pieces I had written. Others with reviews. Another bookcase with books I've reviewed, blurbed, helped the authors in one way or another that was enough to merit a tip of the hat in the acknowledgements. A dedication.

Each book carries its own memories. The expectant opening of a post office box to see if my first self-published book was getting any orders; enough orders to change my life? A university press book dense with pages of notes. My first break-out book with a commercial publisher. A book that sent me on a two week nationwide tour, often with several flights a day to cover different cities in different states. I was much younger then. The reviews, whether perceptive or snarky. The letters and gifts from readers. The occasional award. The terrifying speaking engagements that always turned out to be before enthusiastic audiences. The arrival of royalty statements.

How did I do all this? When did I do it all while gainfully employed in an active career as an attorney?

Writers have given us horrifying glimpses of the most deranged forms of torture in describing the agonies of putting words on paper. Kenneth Roberts said that "childbirth is sheer delirious joy by comparison with the task of wrenching a novel from the brain and transferring it to paper." Rebecca West found writing "a nauseous process," and Gene Fowler has told us that "all you do is sit in a little room and stare at a blank sheet of paper until the drops of blood form on your forehead." Truman Capote called it "a very excruciating life, facing that blank piece of paper every day and having to reach up somewhere into the clouds and bring something down out of them." The prolific Georges Simenon was convinced that "writing is not a profession but a vocation of unhappiness." "Let's face it," William Styron concluded, "writing is hell."

But now, under the oaks on a summer afternoon, I remember none of that. I remember only the joy, the exuberance of taking an idea and working with it, of daily tackling and solving the myriad challenges each chapter, each page, every paragraph can present, of reading over a page that seems just right and adding another page to it, and then another. Of seeing pages accumulate and reading them again and again, with mounting satisfaction and pleasure. Until that day you conclude, reluctantly, after much internal debate, that one of your words, just one, must be changed, just one, and then you will have achieved perfection. Until you realize that a paragraph really should be deleted, and maybe some thoughts re- arranged, and then, eventually, inevitably, you are slashing at your work with a red pen, revising, and realizing you have just made it better. Doing this time and again until at last every thought, every word feels just right. Letting the manuscript sit alone for a while, reading it again, and attacking again, until that fine day when a draft emerges that says exactly what you set out to capture.

For a writer, there is nothing more enjoyable, more engaging, more pleasurable than writing, and those feelings are all I remember now. "The most interesting thing about writing is the way it obliterates time," Gore Vidal remarked; "three hours seem like three minutes." One day melts into another. Hemingway wrote about "how happy" he was "to have put down properly 422 words as you wanted them to be. And days of 1200 or 2700 were something that made you happier than you could believe." Anthony Trollope wrote that "there is perhaps no career of life so charming as that of a successful man of letters . . . Who else is free from all shackles as to hours?" As Annie Dillard declared, "it is life at its most free." John Updike wrote that "Writing is surely a delicious craft, and the writer is correctly envied by others who must slave longer hours and see their labor vanish as they work in the churning of human needs." His son would watch him at night sitting, reading books for reviews or going over proofs with the same stubby golf pencil that recorded his score that afternoon," and noted that he "gave off an impression of leisure and repose, of doing exactly what he wanted to do."

Updike posited that today in the United States, there are perhaps not even one hundred people who can earn a living as a writer without supplementing that income with other work. And therein, of course, lies the rub: making the writing pay.

When I was first starting out, I could write to the editor of any publishing house, from the smallest presses to the largest commercial houses, and get a response back from that editor in a couple weeks at most. It may not have been the response I wanted to hear, but at least I had connected and could keep trying with others. Today, the typical response is simply no reply at all. You sit and wait and hear nothing and not even a gentle follow-up can break the sounds of silence. Today, most of the major commercial publishers will not even make eye contact unless your manuscript is submitted by an agent. Yet today, lining up a literary agency has become an equally frustrating challenge, and a no reply once again has become the typical reply. A month. Two months. Three months. Your carefully worded diplomatic tickler may elicit a few words about what a busy season it is in their publishing cycle and the profound promise "shortly." Month four. Month five. At what point do you toss in the towel? Discouraged and frustrated by the repeated delays in the publication of his first book, twenty-five year old Ernest Hemingway wrote to Ezra Pound: "now we haven't got any money anymore I am going to have to quit writing and I never will have a book published. I feel cheerful as hell. Fuck literature." How many books may we write to "glean our teeming brain" as our productive years dwindle with every delay, every dithering?

Shadows lengthen on the lawn. The insects drone on through the summer afternoon. And in those drowsy hours, shadows of ideas from the last fifty years begin to take shape . . . .

"A SLANT OF WIND"
and
"SOME VAMPIRE EROTICA"

IN AN ESSAY HE WROTE ABOUT *TREASURE ISLAND*, his first successful novel, (which is to say, his first novel which found an audience and made some real money), Robert Louis Stevenson expressed some eternal thoughts about writing. He was thirty-one at the time of his break-through and had written "little books and little essays and short stories, and had got patted on the back and paid for them — though not enough to live upon. I passed my days in toil, the futility of which would sometimes make my cheek to burn, — that I should spend a man's energy upon this business, and yet could not earn a livelihood. Human nature has certain rights," he wrote, "instinct -- the instinct of self-preservation — forbids that any man (cheered and supported by the consciousness of no previous victory) should endure the miseries of unsuccessful literary toil beyond a period to be measured in weeks. There must be something for hope to feed upon."

In short, no one, who doesn't have to, would ever engage in such a maddening enterprise. And you know early on if you have to. It's not a choice.

I grew up in a house with lots of books and parents always reading. I remember being fascinated by the very look of books, and I remember what an impression my paternal grandparents' home had on me when we visited when I was four years old, five, six, seven, walking in the front door of their English Tudor into a chestnut paneled reception hall lined with leaded glass-doored Gothic bookcases, full of books. In the presence of these books, one was filled

15

with awe, as if walking into a cathedral. Most of the other rooms, too, were lined with overflowing bookcases. I remember when my grandfather died, I was seven then, accompanying my father to the house after my grandmother had moved to an apartment, following as he went shelf to shelf, room to room, filling cardboard cartons with books he would bring home and put on his own shelves. And I remember in my father's den, staring, mesmerized, at a book my grandfather had written with his name — which was my name — on the book jacket. *Men and Measures in the Law* by Arthur T. Vanderbilt. I had no idea what that title meant, but there was my name. Someone I knew, someone in my family, had written . . . a book!

So maybe it was inevitable, maybe it was destined, that I wanted to read long before I could read, and when, finally, in first grade, we were taught to read, I sponged it up, eager for more. And that I wanted to write before we were taught to write, how I would pretend to write a book, a few pages with some crayon illustrations, folded and stapled with a cardboard cover.

As Stevenson knew, "the beginner must have a slant of wind, a lucky vein must be running . . . even to begin." If a slant might be not a steady breeze, certainly not a gale, but just a puff or two, well, that was all I encountered. But it was enough, enough when your sails are hoisted and ready to receive any breath of air.

It was in the tenth grade, my first year in senior high school, that I was put in an honors English class with a young, sexy (in my hungry teenage eyes), enthusiastic teacher straight out of Barnard College, who liked my writing and gave me A's and occasionally wrote a comment on something. For a collection of short prose pieces she wrote "Good stuff! This is publishable!," which, in my sophomoric mind, I'm sure I interpreted as meaning publishable in the *The Atlantic* or *The New Yorker*, whereas in retrospect I'm quite certain she meant publishable in the school literary magazine. No matter. Those few words gave me a confidence that kept me going for years. Well into his career, John Updike remembered his high school art teacher who "gave me an underlined 'excellent' in composition; it struck me as an authentic artistic compliment, one of the few I have received."

How gentle need be that slant of wind when all sails are set and trimmed!

In college, my freshman English teacher, near the end of the semester, took me aside and said "you have no idea how good your writing is, do you?" Of course I didn't. How could I? There was no measure of comparison. But his words made me try even harder, to stretch farther, to have some faith in what I was doing, in what I could do. And that made all the difference.

So a simmering desire to write — a book — was always there. And when, in college, the three year interdisciplinary program I was in called for the writing of a senior thesis as the major undertaking of the year, it struck me that one about my grandfather might well be a thesis I could turn into a book, in the same way John F. Kennedy had turned his Harvard thesis into the Pulitzer Prize winning, *Why England Slept*, a book which helped launch his political career. I knew very little about my grandfather other than that he had been a prominent lawyer, president of the American Bar Association, dean of the New York University School of Law, and chief justice of New Jersey — though what those careers and titles really meant was not clear to me. This would be a chance to learn about him, and at the same time better understand what it meant to be a lawyer, since that was the career path I had decided to pursue. And if I could pull it off, it would be the first book written about him.

It worked. The more I delved into his life, the richer the material, the more wonderful became the story. I ended up with a 500 page thesis which was awarded the highest honors in my program, another slant of fair wind which carried me on from there to have faith that this was indeed the start of my first book which, surely, would mark the explosive launch of a brilliant career.

And so began my descent down the rabbit hole into that alternative universe of publishing.

When F. Scott Fitzgerald's first novel, *This Side of Paradise*, was accepted for publication by Scribner's on September 15, 1919, he immediately dashed off a letter to his editor, Maxwell Perkins: "Would it be utterly impossible for you to publish the book Xmas — or, say, February? I have so many things dependent on its success — including of course a girl — not that I expect it to make me a fortune but it will have a psychological effect on me and all my surroundings and besides open up new fields. I'm in that stage where every month counts frantically and seems a cudgel in a fight for happiness against time."

I'm not really sure what all that meant, though I do understand exactly what Fitzgerald was saying. But even the great Perkins' hat full of miracles was limited,and he patiently explained why the book could not appear until, would you believe it, March. So Fitzgerald had to patiently wait six months.

Six months? Six months? A nanosecond! From the time a publisher expressed an interest in my first book until I was holding it took twelve times as long — 48 months — four frustrating, interminable years.

A mere recitation of the tortured time-line this book followed constitutes a presentment of all the elements of a Crime against Humanity at a minimum, and, in all likelihood, a Crime against Nature, too.

It was July 1972. I had graduated from college in May and, ready to conquer the world, was sending inquiries about my proposed book to a host of publishers, when the director of Rutgers University Press expressed an interest and asked that I send him the manuscript when ready. I was spending the summer revising my college thesis, transforming it from thesis to book, and by the end of the summer off it went to Rutgers, which acknowledged receipt of it with a postcard from the "manuscripts editor."

Now, what does a young author know about publishing a book? Back then, nothing. I knew it would take a while to render a verdict on a manuscript and decide whether or not to take on its publication, so I waited patiently, waiting for some word, certainly not about to rock the boat by being pushy, especially since not one of the other publishers I had contacted had expressed a scintilla of interest. After a few months I sent an extremely polite, diplomatic tickler, then another after six months, after eight months, after a year: never a response. After fifteen (15) months, my tickler was not quite as diplomatic and I finally received a postcard from the manuscripts editor stating that "we did secure a reading many months ago and for some reason it was not sent to you." And revealing for the first time that the Press required three independent readers giving their seals of approval before it would take on a book. So fifteen months down the hatch and all to show for it was one reader with a thumbs up. Two to go.

Now being a first time author-in-being, I had not yet learned that it's the worst form of unlucky to talk about your new book until you are cradling it and nursing it in your arms, so I had of course told all my high school and college friends, my professors, my law school friends, neighbors, anyone who would listen, that I was — an author! And my Book was — about to be published!

As month after month went by and these friends asked about it, I began to see the doubt in their eyes, a look which became more pronounced with each passing season, when the look became the one you would use with someone "not quite right" across from you on a deserted midnight subway.

On August 23, 1974, almost two years to the day after the Press had received my manuscript, I was informed by the director of the Press that two more favorable readings of the manuscript had been secured and "I shall assign it to an editor and plan to publish in the Spring of 1975."

OK, a two year detour, but back on track, and all's right with the world. By then I would be graduating from law school, and the publication of my book would help me land a job.

A month later, an editor wrote that he had been assigned my manuscript, and a month after that wrote: "The manuscript is so well written that at present I anticipate only routine editing problems." A week or two later, he wrote again: "From time to time I am going to have questions about the material. I will send these to you in duplicate, and you can indicate your thinking about them on the carbon and return it to me. The first set is enclosed." Wow! This is really getting good! All of my friends, relatives, acquaintances, strangers on the street, received a happy update: publication day, Spring of next year, grows nigh!

But, not so fast: that set of five questions from my editor was to be the first, last, and only set I was to receive for six months. Swiftly fly the years.

Growing concerned, I asked exactly when in the Spring ... fast approaching ... my book was scheduled to appear. At last, in a letter from my editor dated February 12, 1975, I was informed, Surprise! It won't be coming out this Spring after all. "As for when we think the book will be published," he helpfully added, "the only realistic guess I can give you at the moment is in what we call the fall, by which I mean between Labor Day and Christmas." To meet that time frame, he stated, "I'll do everything I can to have the editing completed by March 28."

March 28 came and went with no more communiques from this editor until the end of April when I received some questions regarding the first 20 pages of a 600 page manuscript.

Quite wary by now, in mid May I asked if my book was still scheduled to come out in the fall season; "yes," my editor responded, "we still have your book on our fall list."

Oh really?

Less than a month later, I received a letter from the director of the Press: "It takes us so long to manufacture a book that if it isn't in the hands of our production department by June 1, it has to be held over for the spring list of the following year. And this has happened with your book."

And so it went. Day by day. In the strangest, silliest, most frustrating, most bizarre world I had ever encountered, until, at long last — I'm pretty sure more to get rid of an annoyingly squeaky wheel than for any other reason — a box of books arrived on my doorstep. And no, it of course was not the Spring of the following year. It was the Fall.

Four years to bring the book to publication. In that time, I had entered and graduated from law school and landed my first job, all without the benefit of the book I had thought would help open doors.

Even I recognized that promotion of a book would not be the strong suit of a university press, so I took it upon myself to send out review copies to every conceivable publication that might cover it, from my high school newspaper to the *New York Times*.

The book in fact received generous reviews. The *American Bar Association* predicted that "there will be many readers of this book, and they will be well rewarded." The *American Judicature Society Journal* agreed, saying that "every American lawyer and judge" should read it. *The New Jersey Bar Journal* called it a "well researched volume of lasting worth," and the *Judges Journal* concurred, opining that it "deserves the attention of all in the legal profession." *New Jersey History* found it "indispensable reading" and the *New Jersey*

ArThur T. Vanderbilt II

Law Journal called it "a splendid book." Who could ask for anything more? But despite a mouth-watering potential market of lawyers, judges, law students, despite this glowing coverage, over the course of the year, and verily, over the life of the book, it sold, barely, 500 copies, 100 of which I'm sure I accounted for in my efforts to help push the snowball downhill.

A year after publication, when the book had faded away, I was notified that it had been awarded the Scribes Award of the American Society of Legal Writers, which would be presented at the annual meeting of the American Bar Association. When I researched the Award, I began to think that maybe I had written quite a book after all. It was an award for the best book about the law in a particular year, an award not presented every year, and my predecessors who had won it included such luminaries as Louis Nizer, Paul Freund, Lawrence Friedman, F. Lee Bailey and Richard Kluger, (and some of the recipients in years after me included Gerald Dunne, Richard Posner and G. Edward White, distinguished company to be sure.) My publisher of course did nothing with this news to promote the book, and the Award moved the sales needle not a flicker. If a tree falls in a forest . . .

But the reviews, and this Award, at least were slants of fair wind in my sails which helped me believe that it truly was "them, not me," that my experience with Rutgers University Press had been an aberration and not the norm in publishing a book.

The worst thing an author can do while waiting for publication day, is to sit and wait. Yet the author has invested so much time in the book, the book holds so many hopes and dreams, that it is difficult to do anything but wait. "I should be working, but now I wait for reviews," John Cheever sighed, anticipating the first notices of one of his novels. "I not only wait for them: I write them. I've written them all, even the Albany Times-Union."

It was May of 1975. I had just graduated from law school, for me three years of fog; I empathized with Henry James who told his friend Oliver Wendell Holmes, Jr. that he "sat through the first year's lectures at Harvard Law School and quit in despair because he could not understand, he said, one word of what the lecturer said or what the books said." The fog lifted for me only at the tail end of my law school days, when, suddenly, everything made sense. I could certainly advise someone entering law school — it was a time when this was a popular choice among college graduates, with the nation's law schools accepting some 100,000 eager applicants each year — I could advise them on how to jump in right away with a running start and make the most of their legal education. During a week or two that summer, I typed out everything I knew on my manual typewriter, writing exactly the type of guide that would have made my life a heck of a lot easier.

I had read articles about how this was the type of guide that could be self published and easily promoted and sold, and, still young enough to believe I could build Thoreau's bridge to the moon, I had a plain but serviceable booklet set by our local printer, titled it "How to Succeed in Law School," created my own publishing house, Oak Press, (with nightly dreams of more books to come under this imprint), went to the local bank to set up a business account, walked over to the post office to rent a box (P.O. Box 833), and was ready to go. I forget now all the economics of it — I think I had 1,000 copies run off for what I anticipated would be the "first" printing, and then, in those pre-internet days, wrote a sales pitch piece and a covering letter, and mailed them off to the Career Planning Offices of 1,000 colleges and universities across the country, asking the recipients to post it on their official bulletin board where students would see it. In retrospect, that was a lot of moving parts dependent on a lot of folks doing what I was requesting and not, in their busy lives, just tossing my letter. But mirabile dictu, a week or two later, orders started dribbling in which made me think — for a while — the torrent would soon be coming. Of course, it didn't. And I primed the pump a little more by taking out small ads in college newspapers. Which resulted in another dribble of orders. I think maybe within six months I was coming close to breaking even, but realized this was not going to be the beginning of a great new publishing house.

Just as reality was pushing aside my hopes and dreams, a letter arrived in P.O. Box 833 from a college professor who taught pre-law courses, saying how helpful he had found my manual and placing an order for 200 copies for his classes. Talk about a sudden slant of wind!

With the seal of approval from this very perceptive professor, I was able to interest a law book publisher in bringing out an expanded edition of my manual, which appeared in 1979 as *An Introduction to the Study of Law*, a book which, again, captured in sales some of the gold dust in the stream, but never the mother lode I knew was up in the hills. But this publisher was able to interest a commercial house, Penguin Books, in bringing out a paperback edition. Titled *Law School: Briefing for a Legal Education*, this book included on the cover a blurb from Scott Turow, author of *One L* ("A valuable book for the student contemplating a future in law") and on the back wonderful blurbs from, among others, John Jay Osborne, author of *The Paper Chase* ("A useful tool with which to prepare for the study of law") and the dean of my own law school who must have approved of the insights I was providing into legal education as taught at his school ("I know of no other monograph that would be more helpful to students contemplating the study of law"). I received a $10,000 advance for this book which appeared first in 1981, and which was reprinted thereafter a good number of times.

Quite a lot of mileage, in unexpected ways, from one booklet, which kept the wind in the sails a while longer. Up until this point, my writing had focused on the law — the biography of my grandfather, the law school book, with a colleague in the Attorney General's Office I had edited a three hundred year history of the New Jersey judicial system, and for good measure I had written some articles and book reviews on legal topics. But I was beginning to perceive that the 80,000 some lawyers and judges in New Jersey may not have shared my enthusiasm for legal history, and if they did, they were certainly not buying books. I needed to throw my net further out from shore.

Since childhood I had spent part of every summer on Cape Cod. As a lark, I had written an article about Henry Beston and the year he spent in a cabin on the Cape's outer beach, which resulted in his classic, *The Outermost House*, one of my favorite books. I submitted this to a Cape magazine expecting to hear nothing. Which is exactly what I heard. Until, about eight months later when I received a letter accepting it for publication and enclosing a check for $500. Now this was at a time when, if I received any bi-annual royalty check for any of my books, it was for something like $11.87. I wrote a few more Cape Cod-themed articles for the magazine and was paid $600, $700, $800 for each. Hmmmm. I could read the writing on the wall: time to write something for a non-legal, broader market.

What did I know other than the law? What would be fun to work on for a few years? Certainly something Cape Cod-related would make sense. And since my youngest days, I had had a fascination with pirates. Right at that time, a treasure hunter was searching for a legendary pirate treasure right off the Cape's outer beach; a pirate ship, the *Whydah*, was said to have sunk there in a storm in 1717 with the loss of a fabulous treasure. Fact or fiction, or some of both, I decided to explore this legend of the Cape, and began researching every bit of information I could mine from libraries, historical societies, archives, and contemporary newspapers, and then wrote the story in a manuscript I titled: *Treasure Wreck: The Fortunes and Fate of the Pirate Ship Whydah*.

This was a day — 1985 — when an author could still approach every commercial publisher without an agent, and I sent out inquiries far and wide. A young editor at the venerable publisher, Houghton Mifflin, expressed an interest and asked to see the manuscript, and then, within days, offered a $10,000 advance to take on the book, which I accepted within minutes. (It then, and to this day, amazes me that one major house may have an interest in a book but no others — how can this be? Is it all a matter of hitting the right person at the right time? Whatever, I was a happy camper.)

And my first start-to-finish experience with a commercial publisher was a happy one: it was a pleasure working with my young editor who shepherded my manuscript through all the stages of publication. And in time for Memorial Day, the start of the summer season of 1986, my book was on the market. The enthusiastic director of promotion sent me on a publicity tour focused around Boston and the Cape, with talks, book signings, and radio and television appearances. The book was generously reviewed in all the right spots, the *Boston Herald* serialized the book over several weeks, a condensed book club, *The Select Reader*, included it in its series, and before you could say Labor Day, the first printing of 5,000 copies was gone, a "clean sale" my publishers termed it.

With *Treasure Wreck*, I had proved to myself that I could write commercial nonfiction. And have a great time doing it. Didn't the world need another Walter Lord? Another Barbara Tuchman? An author who could make a living writing well researched, compelling history? I was ready to apply for that job. This was a time when the major publishing houses were paying significant advances, when they were competing with each other to land books with bestselling potential. I was a long way from there but learning enough to realize that the next step up the ladder would be to be represented by a literary agent. But first I needed my next topic.

I had been to Newport, Rhode Island that summer and for the first time had toured The Breakers and Marble House. As I wandered through the rooms, I could hear tourists saying "this is so over the top!" and "how could anyone even live here?" while I was thinking, "man, how great would this be for a party." Somehow, at that point in my life, those relics of the Gilded Age were speaking to me. But who were the people who had lived here? How, in fact, had they lived here? Why had they built these extraordinary monuments to their wealth? When I returned home, I went to our public library and took out a book written by the daughter of the Marble House branch of the family, Consuelo Vanderbilt Balsan's *The Glitter and the Gold*. She had written about growing up in her parents palatial Fifth Avenue mansion, and how terrified she had been as a child each evening after dinner, climbing the grand limestone staircase to her room and sensing ghosts and spirits lurking in the shadows. Suddenly, she became a real person to me, and the more I researched, the more I began to see the human stories behind these mansions. And, wonderfully, no one had yet ventured into this goldmine. I wrote up a thirty page proposal about the book I wanted to write, which I was calling *Fortune's Children: The Fall of the House of Vanderbilt*, and sent it off to a bunch of literacy agencies at a time you could do this and have them actually read it and consider it and at least respond. A couple got back to me, and I signed up with the agent who felt he could get for me the largest advance — in retrospect, perhaps not the best way to make such a decision, but certainly one way.

My agent worked his magic in an auction and in short order had several bids from major commercial publishers. I had been messing around with publishing for ten years and felt a need now to have a break out "big" book, so went with the highest bidder which hit six figures. My agent would take fifteen percent of that advance, as well as fifteen percent of all royalties in perpetuity, but it was worth it: an author on his own could not negotiate this type of deal. He had done his job, he had gotten my editor at William Morrow "completely pregnant" as they say in the trade. To justify, and recover, that sort of advance, the publisher now would have to push the book out the door and sell it on the street corners.

Under my contract with William Morrow, I had eighteen months to submit the completed manuscript. Looking back on that time, I'm not quite sure how I did it while practicing law as a partner in a law firm, with all the time commitments and responsibilities that entailed. But I don't remember feeling any stress during that period; on the contrary, I was so excited by my research, by the story I was uncovering, and by the writing of it, that the months and the work went fast. And at the beginning of Month Number Seventeen, I reported to my agent that I was done and how should I submit the manuscript to my editor: punched into a notebook or loose in a box? He was astounded that I was finished a month ahead of schedule – this was unheard of; he was accustomed to authors begging for extensions, and I could tell by his voice that he was concerned that something was very wrong. "You better send it to me first," he said, ominously, "so that I can see what you've done." The doubts in his voice all but shouted: "my reputation is on the line, punk; you better not have screwed this up." Off to him went the huge manuscript. He called several days later, all the tension drained from his voice: "this is actually much better than I expected. I'll bring it over to Maria myself later this afternoon."

My editor read through the manuscript once, changed just a handful of words, sent it off to the copy editor and the book was scheduled to come out September 1. From receipt of the manuscript on March 1 to book in hand on September 1: that is what a motivated publisher could do. And a lot of good things began happening even before the official publication date. We had gotten a group of nice blurbs from folks like Brooke Astor and John Kenneth Galbraith. The Book-of-the-Month Club and the Literary

Guild had had engaged in a bidding war with the BOMC winning with a bid of over $50,000. A venerable English publisher had purchased the rights for Great Britain for $45,000. On a roll, I had seen an ad for the Reader's Digest's new series of condensed books "*Today's Best Nonfiction*," had shown my agent and asked "how about us?" He contacted the publisher and within a week or two we were signed up and paid $25,000. My publisher had set up a two week nationwide promotion tour for me with stops in all the major cities, to be followed by a ten day book promotion tour of Great Britain. A Dutch magazine was serializing parts of the book as was the *New York Daily News*. And the early reviews coming in were raves. My editor and agent were sure the *New York Times* would treat this as a "big book," meaning it would receive a review in the daily *Times*, and the Sunday *New York Times Book Review* would feature it on the front page.

Neither prediction came to pass. A few days before I was to set out on the publicity tour, my agent called me at the office and with all the clouds of Jove in his voice, read me the review which would appear in a few days in the Sunday *New York Times Book Review*, certainly not on the front page but deep in, and barely half a page at that, a review which damned with faint praise, concluding that there was nothing in the book everyone didn't already know, an opinion which struck me as ludicrous. Not only had there not been a book which dealt with this social history, ever, and had not been, for decades, a book about the Vanderbilt family, but in my research I had discovered in archives parts of the unpublished memoirs of Alva Vanderbilt Belmont — the Vanderbilt wife who ignited the family's building spree — and had drawn on these memoirs, as well as untapped journals and letters, discoveries of which I was proud and which in due course would change how the Gilded Age was viewed. I wrote a "hey, just a minute" letter to the Editors of the Book Review, which of course was never published.

Can a bad review in the *New York Times* kill a book? I'm here to answer that: yes it can. From the appearance of that review and henceforth, my editor never again communicated with me. Ever. The Great Britain publicity tour was cancelled. All behind the scenes work on my book stopped: instantly. And that was that. Just like that. John Cheever reported on his similar experience when his third novel, *Bullet Park*, was picked apart on the front page of the *New York Times Book Review* by Benjamin DeMott, a professor of English at Amherst. "The manuscript was received enthusiastically everywhere," Cheever reported, "but when Benjamin DeMott dumped on it in the *Times*, everybody picked up their marbles and went home." Publishers, editors, agents, are spooked – perhaps they lose faith in their judgment about a book — and scurry away, on to their next book, which maybe will be the big hit they crave.

I was still too inexperienced to be able to connect the dots and comprehend how this one review could stop in its tracks the momentum of a book, but I did have a sense of foreboding. At that stage of a writing career, anything can shake an author's confidence: do I know what I'm doing? or am I a fraud? But it made no logical sense that all the good things that had been happening with the book had been wrong and one snarky review in the *Times* had been right, so on I marched.

In the six months between sending the completed manuscript of *Fortune's Children* to my editor and the appearance of my book, I had researched and written three proposals for my next three books, shooting for a three book contract which, in one stroke, would free me from continuing a legal career and allow me to play Walter Lord, exploring the world and its history rather than filling out timesheets with hours of my life billed to ungrateful clients. As fate would have it, it was a day or two before the appearance of the review in the *Times* that my agent had submitted the three proposals to my editor. I think it was less than 24 hours after the review that he heard back from her: no thank you, no thank you, and no thank you. Boom! When the shooting pain from those blows to the abdomen subsided, I asked him which publishing houses he would try next; "I'm afraid not," was his answer, which had the impact of a knockout punch.

No publisher. No agent. Back to square one. What a very strange business this is, was the thought that consumed me for days, for weeks, after I stumbled home from my two week nationwide promotion tour and took my weary blazer and sport jackets, ties and shirts to the dry cleaners, and waited for something good to happen with the book which would reverse my editor's and agent's throwing in the towel. Surely they would call me and we'd be back on track. Or not.

Had I been more savvy, or had my agent or editor been more nurturing, I would have realized, or they would have suggested, that with *Fortune's Children* I had marked out my field as the Gilded Age, and that it would make eminent sense for my next book to cover something in this period of history as a way of establishing my territory and building an audience. But the necessity of building a brand name never crossed my mind, and what I was interested in at that time was the publishing process, the experiences of other authors which I turned to for ideas and solace. I was pouring through biographies and autobiographies of authors, memoirs of agents, of editors, of publishers, and began to perceive patterns, patterns which not only fascinated me but which I thought would be of interest to readers, both readers who wanted to write, and readers who were interested in authors, of which, I would posit, there is a large number. This became the next topic I would tackle, how a book makes its way from a writer's thoughts to a reader's hand, a manuscript I called *The Making of a Bestseller*. Having no agent, and realizing that this was a difficult topic to sell in a proposal, I decided to write it first and then use the manuscript to line up another literary agency to sell it.

It was a manuscript chock full of shop talk and anecdotes, insights into authors, the creative process, and some of the absurdities of the publishing world which almost all authors have encountered at one time or another. I liked it. A lot.

It was my manifesto, a call to arms: unite authors of the world! We can make this system better!

An agent at the Sterling Lord Agency read the completed manuscript and agreed to represent me, but suggested first that I strip from the manuscript any references to my own experiences as an author, which I did. He then set out to peddle it. The first editor he approached turned him down. "Where to, next?" I asked, and received that same cryptic answer, "I'm afraid that's it."

That's it? What does that even mean? Who are these so-called agents who give up on the first rejection? From the research I had done, I knew how 27 publishers had turned down Dr. Seuss' first classic, 28 had rejected John Grisham's first; 40 passed on the opportunity to publish Nabokov's *Lolita*. All these stories were in my manuscript, did my agent even note the irony? Pifflesticks! I mounted my steed and, like Don Quixote, rushed straight at every publisher out there. All of whom said "pound salt." Except one, a very tiny press in Jefferson, North Carolina — McFarland — which agreed to take it on. My theory at the time was "what does it matter who publishes a book? As long as it's out there and its good, 'they will come.'"

That theory may well be true, though I've never been able to prove it, or even come close. The imprimatur of a known publishing house behind a book can do wonders in jump-starting the success of a book; once again, everyone is looking for that Good Housekeeping Seal of Approval, afraid of trusting their own instincts and judgment and being proved wrong by the market. If a major house is bringing out a book, the presumption is that the "experts" there have vetted it, so it deserves the attention of reviewers, the media, the bookstores and readers. A self-fulfilling prophecy to be sure.

I will say this: the editor assigned to my manuscript at McFarland was, without doubt, the best I had encountered. I would have matched her with anyone at a major house. But I knew promotion is never the strong suit of a small house so again I set out to make a joyful noise unto the world and help jump start the recognition that this book existed. I sent it off to a number of "names" for blurbs, and got back the most wonderful collection imaginable, far better than if I had written them in my dreams:

Judith Appelbaum, the author of the best-selling *How to Get Happily Published*, gave me this one: "It's a joy to take this tour of the book business with its eye-opening emphasis on writers."

Louis Auchincloss opined that "Vanderbilt tells all that every aspiring writer should know about publishing today, and every reader, too."

"Mr. Vanderbilt's book is teaming with lore and advice and warnings and imprecations," wrote William F. Buckley, Jr. "It is a joy as a book to read."

"A blurb —for a man who knows about blurbs and everything else that goes into the making of best sellers, even including the writers thereof," wrote superstar best-selling author Tom Wolfe.

And Frank McCourt had this to say: "Publishing a book is something like going to the track. There's a favorite — but you never know. It's a mystery — though Arthur Vanderbilt's book *The Making of a Bestseller* goes a long way towards penetrating it. Apart from scrutinizing the mystery, Mr. Vanderbilt guides us, with wit and erudition, through the Byzantine world of publishing. Why shouldn't *The Making of a Bestseller* be a bestseller? It's a hell of a good read."

William F. Buckley Jr. was so taken with the book that he devoted a column to it, and when a reader thereafter wrote in, challenging my use of the word "aliteracy" in one chapter, calling the word "an unsightly neologism evidently derived from Greek and Latin in an untutored fashion," Buckley in his reply snapped back at him:

"Oh come on. Language moves, and the movers care not at all if, in search of a useful word, they commit a little etymological miscegenation. And don't say anything against Mr. Vanderbilt because his book, "*The Making of a Bestseller: From Author to Reader*" is splendid and authoritative."

I'll take those seals of approval any day! Who could ask for anything more? Yet my publisher never printed these blurbs on the book, never used them in advertising, or in any sort of promotion. Ever. And sales of the book never even glanced 500 copies.

It was a long time — ten years, a decade — between the publication of *Fortune's Children* in 1989 and *The Making of a Bestseller* in 1999, and someone who is a writer can no more stop seeing stories and conceptualizing books and writing them than a shark can stop swimming forward. In between there was another book which, through the vagaries of the writing, placing, and publication process, came out in 1998. Amy, our beloved golden retriever, had died after sharing ten years with us and I wanted to write a book about our time together. Once again, a difficult book to sell with a proposal — so much would depend on how the book was written, the style, what would make it more than just a book about a household pet? So again I set about to write the book — *Golden Days: Memories of a Golden Retriever* — and once again set out to find a publisher. I lucked upon a perceptive editor at Bantam who offered an advance of $50,000 for the manuscript. Sold America! (Though again one wonders: if a major house like Bantam was ready to take it on, wouldn't — in a rational world — at least a few other commercial houses have an interest? But perhaps that qualification — "rational world" — answers my own question?)

The publication process went well, as one would expect it would with a large commercial house, and good things began happening: a host of blurbs from the likes of actress Betty White to the president of the ASPCA to authors of bestselling books about dogs; a piece about the book in *Town & Country*; an excerpt published in *Reader's Digest*; a large print edition; a German publication of the book; a Chinese edition; a Japanese edition (how about a French edition? a Polish edition; a Yemen edition? you got me), a paperback edition scheduled. All systems for launch were: GO!

And then, just a few days before the official publication date, my editor called. "I have some wonderful news!" he exclaimed.

A brain burst of happiness! Good news! What magical words! A book club bidding war? Another strong foreign sale? Perhaps a British edition? A Hollywood option?

"I'm leaving Bantam at the end of the week," he revealed, "to head up another publishing house!"

Congratulations? Yes, that's certainly wonderful news: for him. But to lose your editor at the moment your book is up at home plate was an unmitigated disaster. You had lost your tender shepherd, you had lost your guardian angel. There was no one else there who cared so much — who cared at all — about the success of your book. "And Megan," he added "will be calling you; she's taking over my list." That call from my editor with his own good news, was the last communication I received from Bantam. The book on its own never earned back the advance, no royalties flowed, a paperback edition came out but had disappeared before you could say "fetch!" (I later was able to interest a smaller press in bringing out a reprint, which has kept the book in print.)

Golden Days was a short book, 143 pages, a memoir which was based on my personal experiences and required almost no research, as contrasted with my earlier books, *Changing Law, Treasure Wreck, Fortune's Children,* and *The Making of a Bestseller,* all of which required serious research. At the time, I was becoming obsessed with gardening, that was my latest passion, my current interest: why not a memoir type of book about what I was doing, what I was experiencing, how I had become a passionate gardener, a gardening addict?

Certainly the market of folks interested in gardening was enormous, but once again this would not be an easy book to sell to a publisher with a proposal; once again it seemed to make sense to write it first, which I did. *Gardening in Eden: Seasons in a Suburban Garden* was the title I gave it and I hoped I had captured in it some universal feelings in my own experiences. This was not a book about gardening any more than *Walden* was book about how to build a cabin in the woods. Once again I made the rounds, starting off with my editor of *Golden Days* who had left to head another publishing house; "So good to hear from you," he responded "but I don't think this will work for our list. So sorry." The same response I heard from every editor at every commercial publisher I tried.

Each inquiry I sent out was tailored to a particular publishing house, sent to an editor there most likely — from his or her track record — to be interested in this book, pointing out comparables, providing evidence of the size of the potential market. Some, of course, sent back form letters that they only considered submissions from agents, though today's favored way of responding seems to be the "no response," even by a senior editor at Simon & Schuster who just had given a colloquium for mid-list authors and encouraged them to submit their proposals to her. I did. And nothing.

This went on for six months, for a year, for eighteen months, to the point where I was running out of publishing houses and was stooping pretty darn low on the food chain, down to houses that brought out books like *How to Grow Geraniums In Your Window*. No one was biting.

One day in the *New York Times* I read a feature article about a new book by Michael Korda, the editor-in-chief of Simon & Schuster, as acclaimed in the second half of the twentieth century as the great Max Perkins had been in the first half. The article was about a new book he had written *Country Matters*, which, in many ways, seemed similar to mine.

Why not? I wrote to him, comparing my book to his, and in an "I ain't got nothing to lose" moment, even mentioned that I had written to one of his senior editors eighteen months before and, as yet, a year and a half later, had heard nothing back from her. Within a few days, there was a letter from Michael Korda, saying "Of course I'd like to read your manuscript; please send it right away."

I did. And several days later received at the office a call from Mr. Korda saying that Simon & Schuster would like to take on my book, he himself would be my editor, and offering an advance of $15,000. Less than I had hoped, but to have Michael Korda as my personal editor, and to have the largest commercial publisher in the United States bringing out my book — when I was at a point I would have gone for no advance with the smallest press headquartered in Anywhere But Here — I jumped at the opportunity. And in abject gratitude to his perspicacity, dedicated my book to him.

Mine, to be sure, was a small book on the Simon & Schuster list for that spring season of 2003, and I'm sure it got only a tiny slice of that season's promotion budget. And the results showed. Other than some great blurbs my editor was able to gather, and a reprint of a small section in *This Old House*, and a large print edition, it staggered along with the sale of only a few thousand copies, not enough to come close to paying off the advance to start the flow of royalties; nor did a subsequent paperback edition help the cause. The few reviewers who took it on seemed to be expecting a "how to" book, which mine was not, and reviewed it for what it wasn't, rather than for what it was. Friends still pose their troublesome gardening questions to me, and when I tell them I don't know the answer, they look confused: "well, you wrote the book about gardening, didn't you?" Well, no, I didn't, and try out on them my *Walden* analogy, at which point they quickly change the subject.

What next? I knew I needed a big book to break out of the doldrums that had trapped my last three books, and thought I had a topic. In researching *The Making of a Bestseller* I kept coming across tantalizing references to an intriguing character named Denham Fouts, who Truman Capote had called "the best kept boy in the world." Denny had been born in Jacksonville Florida in 1914 and by the time he was 19 or 20, had found that his exceptional looks were attracting the attention and devotion of wealthy men, and in the next ten years, his conquests would include a shipping tycoon, the largest landowner in Great Britain, the Crown Prince of Greece who later became King, and one of the wealthiest young men in England. Three famous authors — Christopher Isherwood, Gore Vidal and Truman Capote — all knew Denny and had been so taken with him and his story that they each used him as a character in short stories and novels.

My luck was running: no book had ever been written about Denny, but he made cameo appearances in many memoirs of the times. I had loved Calvin Tomkins classic *Living Well is the Best Revenge*, his short book about Sara and Gerald Murphy, the American ex-patriots who lived in France after World War I and befriended such young Americans as F. Scott Fitzgerald, Ernest Hemingway and Cole Porter, a book which had been serialized in *The New Yorker* and was a strong bestseller. *Living Well is the Best Revenge* is a literary footnote, focused on two little known, minor characters, who the author brought to life in a larger context. I thought I could do the same with Denny's story. Capturing such an elusive character as Denny Fouts was similar to trying to capture Captain Bellamy, the pirate captain in my book *Treasure Wreck*, and I spent a good ten years tracking clues and tracing him, searching books and memoirs and diaries, anything for snippets of information, scouring archives here in the United States and abroad, even under the Freedom of Information Act seeing if the FBI had any files on him, reaching out to anyone still alive who knew him or might have a photo, a letter, anything. In my search, I made some major finds, discovering a partial draft novel in his own handwriting that Denny had been working on, fragments of a diary he kept at one time, a few postcards, as well as enough information to piece together his story for the first time. It was so strange a story, a wonderful tale, and in my 155 page book *"Best-Kept Boy in the World"* about the same length as the 148 pages of *Living Well is the Best Revenge*, I think I captured Denny and his unusual life, as well as the intersecting worlds of Isherwood, Vidal and Capote.

Over the years, I had come to know the author Edmund White, and I sought his advice as to the literary agent he would recommend for this book. He referred me to one who had a hot hand and whose life story was similar to Denny's. The agent gave the manuscript a read and said "no thank you" as did a few others before I once again started the rounds of floating it by different publishers.

The trouble today with everything computerized is that any editor can, with the click of a few computer keys, check out the sales records of your past books, and if they are anything but stellar, that is the end of the story. If a book hasn't earned its advance, it seems an easy business decision, and perhaps a wise one, not to throw good money after bad; and it's an easy way to make a decision without having to use your own judgment as to the merits of the new manuscript before you.

I kept in touch with Edmund White as to my progress, or lack thereof, and after a stretch in the wilderness where he could see nothing was happening and that nothing was going to happen, he referred me to a good friend who was an editor at Riverdale Books, who accepted the manuscript as soon as he read it. Riverdale is a small press, and by now I knew the chances of a book reaching the audience for which it was intended were slim to none with a small press, but hope for an author does indeed seem to — must — spring eternal, and once more I felt that it was better to have the book out there and to see what the market would do, than to have the manuscript sitting in a drawer.

Riverdale was in the process of transition at this time, absorbing another publisher and transforming its business model to try to shave costs. As a result, my book, slated to come out a certain date, was pushed back in the publishing schedule.

I was used to all this and realized I had no choice, so sat and waited patiently. It finally made its appearance in the fall of 2015, a good four years after it had been accepted. When accepted for production in 2012, the book was to be a hardcover; these plans were scrapped to save money; it would come out as a paperback, a decision which insured that most/all publications would not review it. An index was eliminated, a decision which — in the eyes of many — makes a nonfiction book of questionable value. And a notebook of irreplaceable photographs I had Federal Expressed to my editor were lost in the shuffle and never found. (A number of Amazon "reviewers" noted that the book would have been much better had it included photographs. You think?)

With no bargaining power, you stay in the ring and take the pounding and try not to lose consciousness, always with the thought: the book is at least out there; it will find its market. Well, no, not really, except, perhaps, in rare circumstances. The publishers never sent the book out for blurbs. It was never reviewed. There was a bit of film interest in the story, as well there should have been; if the movie "Capote" was a huge hit and award winner, Denny's story was many times more inherently fascinating, but nothing ever came to fruition. Sales have probably repaid my costs; but for the ten years I devoted to the book, I would have made much more money bagging groceries. Such are the glories of authorship.

So passed forty years messing around in the world of writing and publishing with its maddening brew of unexpected defeats and out-of-the-blue victories. Who, but a masochist, or someone who had to write, would continue on? I had retired from the practice of law and now could devote all of my time to my obsession.

But the slant of wind? Where was that necessary slant of wind?

Inevitably, eventually, does it come? Not something you can bank on, but it did. In a gale-like blast. My book *Fortune's Children: The Fall of the House of Vanderbilt* had been published in 1989 by Morrow and since then I had received bi- annual royalty checks, not large, but, nevertheless nice to have a book perking along long two decades, after its debut. This was, after all, the ultimate goal of writers — to have a stable of books that, like pensions, would provide a flow of funds for years to come. And then, after Morrow had been subsumed by Harper Collins, a wise executive there must, one day, have wondered how to keep a roomful of bright young interns productively occupied and suggested that they go see if they could squeeze any more profits from the backlist. An exceptionally bright intern must have been assigned to my book, and designed a new cover. And on the front of the cover, in stand-out print, etched seven magic words: "The Vanderbilts — The Real-Life Downtown Abbey."

This was in December of 2012, a time when "Downton Abbey" had achieved a cult status of must-see TV. The editor who had been assigned to my book sent me a copy. It looked nice. And it looked even nicer four months later when I got my first royalty check since the issuance of this new edition and it had increased. Increased by a factor of twelve! A trend which continued when the next statement was received, and the next and the next. (One wonders why this waiting market could not have been tapped in the prior decades, but one tries not to be ungrateful when the wind finally picks up).

Reef the sails! Lower the jib! A gale now was blowing!

Pretty much every year since publication in 1989, the film rights for *Fortune's Children* had been under option for a film or television movie. As is usually the case with such options, nothing ever panned out. But the option income did allow me to remodel my kitchen and to start building up a pension/profit sharing plan. And then during the height of the *Downtown Abbey* craze, a call from Lionsgate to option the property to develop the American version of "*Downtown Abbey*," it would be a five or six season series that would develop the characters and story in the same way the *Downtown Abbey* story was unfolding. A Dream Team of producers, directors and screenwriters was assembled, we met for lunch at the Hotel Carlyle in New York City, we strategized, we found we were all on the same page, and as we got up to leave we all but gave the war whoops of a hyped up football team jogging onto the field.

Time to pyramid this great news! Working in overdrive in the Freedom of Retirement, I had just finished two manuscripts, one nonfiction, the other my first novel, and had been pondering how to place them. This, now, was going to be a piece of cake.

I contacted the editor at Harper Collins who had been assigned my book *Fortune's Children*, and told her all the good news — how the new cover and the new handle were increasing sales so dramatically that this success story could be used in her publishing house to illustrate the value of a back list, topped by the news of the forthcoming miniseries of the next *Down Abbey*. "Wonderful," she said when I told her about my just completed manuscripts, "please send them along."

I did, and slept soundly with visions of sugar plums dancing in my head. For the first week.

But then the second week came and went. And the third. And the fourth. Six weeks. She was not responding to my super polite email ticklers. Until at last she realized she had to respond. "I enjoyed reading them," she said, "but there is really not a place for them on my list. Right now I'm looking for Vampire Erotica. Do you have anything in that category?"

And so it goes. After almost a half century of mucking around with books, the process of bringing one to fruition, of finding an audience, hasn't gotten any easier, and, truth be told, has become increasingly bizarre. Vampire erotica?

As Hemingway wrote in the preface to the collection of his first forty-nine short stories: "Now it is necessary to get to the grindstone again. I would like to live long enough to write three more novels and twenty-five more stories. I know some pretty good ones." I do, too. And if I can catch a fair slant of wind, I'll pull in the sails and steer onward to try, once again.

From
"SEND ME A MAN WHO READS"
to
"WHO READS TODAY? SEND ME A WIDE RECEIVER"

I REMEMBER IN JUNIOR HIGH SCHOOL — back in the early 1960s — thinking about going to college, regarding it as a distant, grown-up world alien to anything I had ever known. And I remember in those days being captivated by a full page advertisement that appeared quite frequently in popular magazines. "SEND ME A MAN WHO READS" was the headline of these ads run by the International Paper Company. The ones I remember well featured a college student sitting under a tree in a bucolic campus setting, engrossed in a book. Its purpose, in addition, I suppose, to promoting the importance and use of paper, was to foster the idea that colleges, and later, employers, were looking for the sort of person who was passionate about reading, about books — as I was — because that passion was indicative of something so central, so core, that it said perhaps everything about who the person was. And what it said was good. Very good indeed.

Within a few years, these ads, still with the same headline, featured a collegiate-type reading under a tree near a pond, but now with this helpful assurance added for concerned parents: "If your boy reads a lot, don't worry about his becoming a bookworm. New research by International Paper shows that top scholars are also likely to be athletes and leaders."

Phew! Thank goodness for that new research which must have helped dispel many a concerned parent's worst nightmares.

Perhaps that belated addendum was a sign even way back then that the times they were a'changing. Today, if a college or university were to be honest, it would run an ad — politically correct, to be sure — that reads: "Send Me a Person Who . . . Excels in Football," or Basketball, or Lacrosse, or fill in the blank with whatever the school's athletic department needed at the moment to create a winning team to bring in the most revenue.

For institutions of "higher learning" are certainly not reticent about trumpeting their new wish list. The *New York Times* of January 27, 2014 ran a front page article, above the fold, accompanied with a three column photograph, entitled "Committing to Play for a College, Then Starting 9th Grade," featuring a ninth grade soccer star from Sanford, Florida and the sixteen (16) college soccer coaches from sixteen (16) colleges and universities pursuing her. Before she entered the ninth grade, she had been offered full scholarships from several. The article reported that this early recruiting was not limited to one student, or one sport, but also covered middle school boys who excelled in football and basketball, and girls who stood out from their teammates in lacrosse, volleyball and field hockey. One student reported having phone conversations with college coaches "nearly every night during the eighth grade." Coaches at Ivy League schools put their favorite young sports stars on a special list of preferred candidates to be slipped to the admission officer of their institutions, and reported that they were instructed by their admission officers to consider students with lower grade point averages and test scores than required for non-athlete applicants.

These *colleges,* these *universities,* are kidding us with all this, right?

Apparently not.

Should we be waiting for the front page feature article in the *New York Times* about college recruiters pouring over eighth grade literary magazines and school newspapers to spot the outstanding poet, the exceptional writer? Attending middle school science fairs to search out the brilliant adolescent scientist? Sitting through eighth grade productions of "Our Town" and "Guys and Dolls" to spot the stand-out thespian? Monitoring eighth grade math classes to be awed by thirteen year old Einsteins? Observing school election campaigns to spot the best leaders?

Don't hold your breath.

Put aside the fact that, as the article reported, many of these young recruits disappoint when they finally arrive at the college or university so obsessed with them, and end up spending four years on the bench. On full scholarships. The truly baffling question — never raised — is why no one, no one today is saying "Hey, wait just a minute! What exactly is the purpose of a college education?"

If it is to turn out high school soccer coaches, then these recruiting colleges are doing a splendid job.

But what happened to their quest for the man who reads?

What happened to the day when colleges required of every student at least a semester on Western Civilization? Today not one of the top fifty colleges has such a mandate.

What happened to those days when I was in junior high school when we studied Homer's *Odyssey*, and Shakespeare's *Julius Caesar*, and Thoreau's *Walden* — and not "young adult" versions, not dummy-downed texts, and certainly not "graphic novels" (omg — has it really come to this?) — the original texts of books that then were considered a foundation of our civilization and not yet mocked as a curriculum of dead white men, books that are the common thread of a diverse population, the key to understanding each other and our worlds, books that would probably never be read, or understood, except in a classroom setting? What happened to those days, to that steadfast belief in the importance of reading, of a liberal arts education?

For the evidence is overwhelming that readers are just not out there today. And those that are, are not only no longer coveted. By anyone. They are no longer even relevant.

The evidence of this sea change is as overwhelming as it is disheartening. Much as we would like to consider ourselves a civilized and literate people, there is a staggering mass of evidence to the contrary.

According to the 2010 census, the population of the United States is 308 million, with an average age of 36.8 years. That's a lot of people of reading age. But selling books in the United States is like selling "apps" in a country where 75 percent of the population doesn't own an iPhone, and the 25 percent of the population that does, hasn't a clue how to use them or a desire to try.

In a slow season, the sale of 50,000 books may be enough to propel a new title onto the national best-sellers list, the sale of 300,000 to 700,000 enough to reach the fabled number one spot. The sale of one million books over the course of a year, representing a readership of less than one half of one percent of the American public, constitutes a runaway best-seller.

Such figures have not changed all that much from what they were almost a century ago — in 1923, for instance, when Walter Page, one of the founders of Doubleday Page, bemoaned the fact that "the masses even of intelligent folk have yet hardly fairly begun to buy books. Go where you will among the people and you will find few books — pitifully few."[1] The ten best-selling novels in the period from 1919 to 1927 sold from 140,000 to 814,000 copies each, with the top nonfiction titles in the period ranging from 44,000 to 1,000,000, not too far from today's puny figures. Keep in mind that the population of the United States in 1925 was 110,000,000 — about one-third what it is today. John Steinbeck was always amazed that the print run for one of his books in Denmark, with a population then of 5 million, would be just about the same size as the print run for the United States, with a population in his day of 130 million. Publishers and agents consider 25,000 copies to be a sensational sale for a new book. How can this be?

According to a study conducted in 2014 by the U.S. Department of Education and the National Institute of Literacy, thirty-two million adult Americans — fourteen percent of our population — cannot read or write, period. Twenty-one percent of adults are functionally illiterate, cannot read a help wanted ad or recipe, write a check or address an envelope.[2] It is estimated that sixty-three million adult Americans can't read or write beyond an eighth grade level. This number is said to be increasing by 800,000 to one million each year. A 1993 survey released by the Department of Education found that ninety million Americans over the age of sixteen do not have the most basic reading and writing skills required for employment.[3] Every eight seconds of every school day, an American student drops out of school. Every year, 700,000 students graduate without the ability to read their diplomas.[4] Was there any surprise when a report funded by the National Endowment for the Arts found that literate reading has been declining among young adults during the last two decades?[5] Or when a survey by the National Endowment for the Humanities revealed that more than half of all college seniors flunked a basic history and literature test?[6]

Illiteracy gets all the press, but just as disturbing a problem is aliteracy, which has been defined as the ability to read without the desire to do so. This affliction, even among high school and college graduates, is rampant.

How common it is, nowadays, to walk into a home, decorated as if *Architectural Digest* had just completed a six-page photo spread, and feel something wrong, something missing: not a book in the house, not a book to be seen anywhere.

These poor people, first of all, are missing out on a great decorating technique; novelist Paul Horgan called a wall of books "the most pleasingly decorative side for a room after a mural painting or a tapestry by master hands."[7] As James Michener has written, it is the concept of a book itself that is "one of the finest symbols of our civilization."[8] And these poor folk are also missing out on making their homes come alive, for, as Cicero said, "a room without books is a body without a soul."[9] There is something about just having the books there. "Books are a delightful society," William Gladstone wrote. "If you go into a room filled with books, even without taking them down from their shelves, they seem to speak to you, to welcome you."[10]

These people are, of course, missing out on something much more. (A developer who is building on spec in Los Angeles, a 100,000 square foot home with an asking price of $500 million, easily solved the problem of what to do with the double height glass walled library: "Nobody really reads books," he said, "so I'm just going to fill the shelves with white books, for looks." A solution which, for any reader, will bring back memories of Jay Gatsby's library with its shelves filled with books whose pages had never been cut.) [11] Better to read the books than just to have them on the shelves, for reading provides more opportunities for happiness than are available to someone who has never discovered its joys. It is a way of experiencing life, of altering perceptions, thereby increasing the range and richness of our lives. As S.I. Hayakawa put it, "In a very real sense, people who have read good literature have lived more than people who cannot or will not read. . . It is not true that we have only one life to live; if we can read, we can live as many more lives and as many kinds of lives as we wish."[12]

Think of your favorite books, the ones you enjoyed when you read them, the ones you didn't want to put down; the ones you

thought about after you finished them. These are the books you take off
the shelf to reread every few years, the ones you open to certain pages to read and read again. Think of the characters that you remember
as vividly as you remember anyone you've ever known: Huck Finn, Jim
Hawkins, Scarlett O'Hara, Holden Caulfield, Jean Brodie, Mr. Chips,
Ebenezer Scrooge, Tony Fry, Jay Gatsby, Phineas, Scout Finch, Holly
Golightly. "My library," wrote Shakespeare in *The Tempest*, "was duke-
dom large enough." There are people out there, educated people, many
people, who have never met Huck or Holly. One wonders sometimes
how they live without having made such acquaintance. A Parisian host-
ess once asked Benjamin Franklin his thoughts on what condition of
man most deserved pity. After due reflection, Franklin responded: "A
lonesome man on a rainy night who does not know how to read."[13]

The failure to impart the joys of books and reading to more people is the most woeful failure of our educational system, from first
grade through college, (and of publishers, who have thus failed to
further their business interests). Reading is the foundation of all education, and education still, now, and always, is the best, and only,
hope for solutions to all the problems society faces.

If the American people are not reading, what are they doing?

Every day not too many years ago, 73 percent of all American
thirteen- year-olds watched three or more hours of television. Today
sacred iPhones and iPads, Facebook, Twitter and that morass called
"Social Media" consumes on average almost two hours a day. Reading and writing scores on the Scholastic Aptitude Test fell dramatically in the 1970s — across socioeconomic groups — and have never
recovered. The College Board which sponsors the SAT, attributed
the continuing decline in verbal scores to an erosion of reading time.

Stated Donald Stewart, the president of the College Board:
"Reading is in danger of becoming a lost art among too many American students."[14]

There is an even scarier statistic: that 90 percent of everyone in the United States spends one third of their waking hours watching television. About 500,000 Americans would go out and buy a Judith Krantz hardcover novel, while 20,000,000 people would turn on their television sets to watch the same Judith Krantz novel turned into a mini-series. (As James Michener said late in his life: "If I were a young man today, I think I would head toward Hollywood and the movies. That medium is so effective and commands an immense audience. I would think that none of my books ever came within 3 percent of the audience that a Spielberg movie gets, and that counts for something."[15]). When Johnny Carson was its host, twelve million Americans tuned in every night to watch the Tonight show; forty-five million viewers watched his final show. Forty- two million viewers watched Ellen DeGeneres come out on her weekly sitcom. Thirty- eight million viewers saw sitcom character Murphy Brown have her baby. Thirty-six million Americans regularly watched Roseanne. Each year, the Superbowl is watched on television by well over one hundred million Americans and hundreds of millions more viewers worldwide. So anxious are advertisers to reach this audience that they will pay five million dollars for thirty seconds of air time. Truly here, in these exalted hours, is today's shared American experience.

In New York City alone, there are estimated to be 250,000 heroin addicts. Are there 250,000 book buyers? Are there 250,000 book readers? As Gore Vidal repeatedly noted, "The audience for the novel is demonstrably diminishing with each passing year."[16] His estimate that only 3 to 5 percent of our population reads books seems on the mark.

Critic Christopher Lehmann-Haupt asked Jack Shoemaker, the editor-in- chief of North Point Press in Berkeley, California, how many serious readers are out there. "I'm not certain that there is such a thing as a general serious literary audience," he responded. "If there is, it surely is not above 15,000 people in this country . . ."

Lehmann-Haupt pressed: Is this audience growing or contracting? "I think it's steadily getting older, and it shows no signs of growing. And I think that a quick survey of some of the big independent booksellers will confirm my sense that there is no meaningful audience in their teenage years or people in their twenties. These stores are largely supported by people in their late thirties to mid-fifties." Novelist Philip Roth's assessment is just as grim: "There's been a drastic decline, even a disappearance, of a serious readership," he has said; "we are down to a gulag archipelago of readers."[17] "It is a mistake to think that books have come to stay," E.M. Forster once said. "The human race did without them for thousands of years and may decide to do without them again."[18]

Truly the barbarians are not only at the gates; they have breached the gates. They are among us. They are us. As Eugene Ionesco simply put it: "People who don't read are brutes."[19]

Today, who reads? According to the numbers, those who do are so rare and such a curiosity that they might just as well be enlisted in a carnival sideshow exhibit.

Woe unto him who reads too often, or admits he does it at all. During his confirmation proceedings, Supreme Court Justice David Souter was made out to be some sort of freak because of his reading habits. "To call Souter bookish would be like describing the Grand Canyon as a hole in the ground," *Time* analogized. "In the ramshackle farmhouse nine miles outside Concord where he has lived since he was 11, groaning shelves of books on philosophy, history and the law have won the battle for space. Vacations are devoted to rereading as much of the work of a particular author as he can; he has plowed through Dickens, Proust, Shakespeare and Oliver Wendell Holmes. . ." Certainly there was something suspect about all of this. Despite *Time's* report that while a Rhodes scholar at Oxford, Souter and a group of friends "would return so late to their rooms after visiting the local pubs that they would have to climb a ladder to get over the locked gates" and that friends at Harvard Law School reported that no one they'd ever met "is more fun at a party," *Time* pondered what it considered a serious issue: "whether a man who seems to prefer books to people can empathize with and understand the problems of ordinary people."[20] Flash back a hundred years or so, and David Souter's reading habits would have been the stuff of legend, especially if he read beside a fire in a log cabin.

Gore Vidal has recounted a story that illustrates just how much the reading habits of our society have changed in those hundred years:

> For some years 1 have been haunted by a story of [William Dean] Howells and that most civilized of all our presidents, James A. Garfield. In the early 1870s Howells and his father paid a call on Garfield. As they sat on Garfield's veranda, young Howells began to talk about poetry and about the poets that he had met in Boston and New York. Suddenly, Garfield told him to stop. Then Garfield went to the edge of the veranda and shouted to his Ohio neighbors. "Come over here! He's telling about Holmes, and Longfellow, and Lowell, and Whittier!" So the neighbors gathered around in the dusk; then Garfield said to Howells, "Now go on."

> Today we take it for granted that no living president will ever have heard the name of any living poet. This is not, necessarily, an unbearable loss. But it is unbearable to have lost those Ohio neighbors who actually read books of poetry and wanted to know about the poets.[21]

People today — public people certainly — are reluctant even to admit that they *read*. Bill Moyers once quoted the poet *Joseph* Brod*sky* as having said that "you can tell a great deal more about a candidate for the presidency from the last book he read than the last speech he gave."[22] In his first presidential campaign, the first George

Bush told the approving American public that he didn't read many books. In a profile in *The New Yorker* of his closest advisor, Secretary of State James Baker, it was reported that Baker "is not much of a reader. 'His outlet is turkey hunting, not books,'" his pastor noted.[23] As Gore Vidal hinted, perhaps it's better that way. Vice President Dan Quayle presented his book reports to doubtful reporters as proof that he had read books: "I read Nixon's book, 1999 . . . Nixon's book was about the Soviet Union and how we ought to handle them in the future, in 1999."[24] President Trump has declared his favorite book to be his own, *The Art of the Deal*, which was written by a ghostwriter.

Compare all this to John F. Kennedy, who turned his Harvard senior thesis into a best-seller: *Why England Slept*; who, while recovering from a back operation, wrote *Profiles in Courage*, another bestseller and winner of the Pulitzer Prize for biography; who brought historian Arthur Schlesinger, Jr., to the White House to advise on the historical precedents of current political problems; who was a speed reader devouring books by the bushel; who recommended to his staff books like Barbara Tuchman's *The Guns of August*. Similarly, President Obama found during his eight years in office, "a time when events move so quickly and so much information is transmitted," that reading for an hour each night gave him the ability to "slow down and get perspective" and "the ability to get in somebody else's shoes." He found, for instance, how Shakespeare's tragedies have been "foundational for me in understanding how certain patterns repeat themselves and play themselves out between human beings." His goal out of office is to use his presidential center website "to widen the audience for good books" and encourage a public "conversation about books."[25]

The regard that today's society affords to authors is just about the same it affords to readers. Aspiring writers may live on fantasies of glory, but in real life, the glory is not there.

Where are the Oscars, the Emmys, the Tonys, the Grammys for authors? Where is that special television extravaganza to honor our best writers? Nowhere. In fact, there are no television programs about books. From 1975 until 1990, France had a weekly ninety-minute television show, *Apostrophes*, featuring authors discussing their latest books, a show that in France achieved the popularity that *Wall Street Week* had in the United States. "America is basically anti-intellectual," novelist William Styron said, explaining why such a show wouldn't succeed here. "My own feeling is that Americans in general have so little regard for serious literature that a TV book show could never achieve truly wide popularity."[26] Nan Talese, editor at Doubleday, agreed: "Americans aren't French, and we don't get excited about ideas."[27] In fact, when Johnny Carson's *Tonight Show* was cut back in 1980 from ninety minutes to an hour, it was authors who first disappeared as his guests. The *New York Times* each day includes a review of one book, while running a Sports Section of six or more pages. (On Sunday, of course, there is the Book Review, but there also is a beefier Sports Section.)

Annie Dillard has written that an author may excite in his fellow man "not curiosity but profound indifference. It is not my experience that society hates and fears the writer, or that society adulates the writer. Instead my experience is the common one, that society places the writer so far beyond the pale that society does not regard the writer at all."[28] Saul Bellow humorously recalled his encounters with politicians:

American writers are not neglected, they mingle occasionally with the great, they may even be asked to the White House but no one there will talk literature to them. Mr. Nixon disliked writers and refused flatly to have them in, but Mr. Ford has invited them together with actors, musicians, television newscasters and politicians. . . . Questions of language or style, the structure of novels, trends in painting are not discussed. The writer finds this a wonderful Pop occasion. Senator Fulbright seems almost to recognize his name and says, "You write essays, don't you? I think I can remember one of them." But the Senator, as everyone knows, was once a Rhodes Scholar.

It is actually pleasant on such an evening, for a writer to pass half disembodied and unmolested by small talk from room to room, looking and listening. He knows that active public men can't combine government with literature, art and philosophy. Theirs is a world of high-tension wires, not of primroses on the river's brim. Ten years ago Mayor Daley in a little City Hall ceremony gave me a five hundred dollar check on behalf of the Midland Authors' Society. "Mr. Mayor, have you read *Herzog?*" asked one of the reporters standing by. "I've looked into it," said Daley, yielding no ground."[29]

There once was a day when Americans lined up on the wharves of Boston and New York awaiting the ships from England that would deliver the latest installment of Charles Dickens' *The Old Curiosity Shop*, a day when Thomas Paine's *Common Sense* sold 100,000 copies in ten weeks, when Longfellow's *The Courtship of Miles Standish* sold 10,000 copies in twenty-four hours. There once was a day when reading was a popular form of entertainment, when books provided a shared experience for a diverse and fragmented population.

Amazed publishers are reminded time and again that that day has gone, that their franchise slipped away from them while they weren't minding the store. "You publish a book under the notion that there are people who will share your tastes, share your enthusiasm," Sonny Mehta, the head of Knopf, once said. "It's disheartening to find that, apart from the fellows in the office, there's potentially only a handful — 3,000, 4,000, 5,000 people — in the country."[30] Lawrence Henry Gipson's volumes of history concerning *The British Empire Before the American Revolution* received the most extraordinary praise and yet were selling fewer than one thousand copies per volume. "I am tempted to raise my hands above my head," exclaimed their dismayed publisher, Alfred A. Knopf, "expose my galluses, and exclaim in the immortal words of that great border-state keynoter: How long, America! Oh how long, America! Oh how long! "[31]

Clearly, a commercial publisher like Knopf, will not, cannot, take on a book which will have such weak sales.

Which forces the authors of such extraordinary books into the hands of smaller publishers. If they can even find a small publishing house which will get behind their book.

Which makes it even harder for those readers who may be interested in such a book to learn of its existence.

With the resulting anemic sales making it even more difficult for the next book by this author, or of this nature, to find a publisher, or an audience.

What to do?

In his classic essay, *On the Need for a Quiet College* that explored the purpose of a higher education, Stephen Leacock wrote that "The proper studies for my college are history and literature and philosophy and thought and poetry and speculation, in the pursuit of which each [student] shall repeat the eager search, the unending quest of the past. Looking for one thing, he shall find another. Looking for ultimate truth, which is unfindable, they will learn at least to repudiate all that is false." Leacock's students would not focus their studies on preparing for a trade, a profession, a sport, a business; they simply would learn to think. Each of Leacock's professors would be "a magician — with such an interest and absorption in a topic that those who listened would catch the infection of it, hurry from the lecture to the library, still warm with thought."[32]

Would hurry from the lecture hall to the library to what? To read a book. Is this too quaint an idea in a day when if a class is to study, perchance, Thoreau, it will be a class called "Thoreau and Global Warming"? While Governor of California, Ronald Reagan cut spending for the University of California system noting that the taxpayers should not be "subsidizing intellectual curiosity." Could it be that that is exactly what we should be subsidizing? Leacock's essay was published in 1938. How close his reasoning was to the conclusion almost 60 years later in Frank Bruni's essay in the *New York Times*, "College, Poetry and Purpose," which highlighted his favorite college professor who proposed that a college's mission "is for developing the muscle of thoughtfulness, the use of which will be the greatest pleasure in life and will also show what it means to be fully human."[33]

As colleges and universities continue to build winning teams, as reading falls by the wayside and we descend in today's disheartening illiteracy/aliteracy death spiral, we can only pray for deliverance, that someday, some educator will awaken and recognize that "quaint" may be good, that "quaint" works, and once again run an ad: "Send me someone, anyone, who reads."

THE BAFFLING CASE OF F. SCOTT FITZGERALD

And the Mystery of Best-Sellers

HOW A BOOK MAKES ITS WAY from an author's head to a reader's hand has always been shrouded in mystery.

While editor-at-large at Macmillan, Edward Chase once commented that it was his experience that if writers are really determined to get published, "if they really stick at it, eventually — like salmon swimming upstream — they're going to make it. But it takes determination and endurance."[1]

Really?

The sagas of such upstream journeys are often a downright scary testament to the vagaries of chance, to the arbitrariness of rejection, to the luck of acceptance and strong sales. What would your advice be to people who want a career in writing? Harper Lee once was asked. "Well, the first advice I would give is this: hope for the best and expect nothing. Then you won't be disappointed."[2]

Good advice is often hard to accept. The reason many don't immediately recognize the wisdom of Miss Lee's words perhaps may be traced to a mystery which began on a warm summer evening in July of 1918 when twenty-one-year-old Scott Fitzgerald met eighteen-year-old Zelda Sayre, that captivating, Southern belle tomboy who was already sneaking a smoke, a drink of corn liquor, and necking; Zelda, who had been voted the "prettiest and most attractive" girl in the Montgomery, Alabama, high school graduating class.

Or, to be more exact — as Fitzgerald was — the case began to unfold when he "fell in love on the 7th" of September, as he noted in his journal,[3] and concluded that to win the hand of this "whirlwind" he had to draw on his "ace in the hole" and complete the novel he had been spinning in his head.[4]

To be even more precise about it, the clues became tantalizing when his sophomoric scheme worked: when his novel was accepted for publication and was an instant hit.

Before he took leave of his senses and dreamed up this plan to win Zelda, Scott Fitzgerald had been working for ninety dollars a month with the Street Railway Advertising Company, "writing the slogans that while away the weary hours in rural trolley cars,"[5] finding in this humdrum world that "all the confidence I had garnered at Princeton and in a haughty career as the army's worst aide-de-camp melted gradually away."[6] With a sense that time was running out, he quit his advertising job, left New York City and "crept home"[7] to St. Paul, Minnesota, announcing to his family that he was going to write a novel. "Through two hot months I wrote and revised and compiled and boiled down."[8] It seemed never once to have crossed Fitzgerald's mind that his book, like just about every first novel, was destined to oblivion. "This is a definite attempt at a big novel and I really believe I have hit it," Fitzgerald wrote on July 26, 1919, to Max Perkins, a young editor at Scribner's, the publishing house Fitzgerald hoped would accept his manuscript. "Now what I want to ask you is this — if I send you the book by August 20th and you decide you could risk its publication (I am blatantly confident that you will) would it be brought out in October, say, or just what would decide its date of publication?"[9]

The novel was mailed off to New York City at the end of the summer, and Fitzgerald, "an empty bucket, so mentally blunted with the summer's writing," had taken a job repairing car roofs at the Northern Pacific shops.[10]

Suddenly, on September 15, 1919, the postman rang. A special delivery letter. And there he goes! Look! There goes Scott, now F.

Scott Fitzgerald, running "along the streets, stopping automobiles to tell friends and acquaintances about it — my novel, *This Side of Paradise*, was accepted for publication." [11]

Fitzgerald was pretty oblivious to the nature of the miracle that had just befallen him, pressing Perkins to get the book out at once. Zelda was almost trapped in his net. The day he received word of his book's acceptance by Scribner's, he dashed off a note to Perkins: "Would it be utterly impossible for you to publish the book Xmas — or, say, by February? I have so many things dependent on its success — including of course a girl." [12] But even Perkins' hat full of miracles was limited, and he patiently explained why the book could not appear until — would you believe it — March. Fitzgerald understood. "I feel I've certainly been lucky to find a publisher who seems so generally interested in his authors. Lord knows the literary game has been discouraging enough at times." [13] My, my, at twenty-two. Wait a few years Scott; you ain't seen nothing yet!

The acceptance of *This Side of Paradise* had been anything but inevitable. One of Scribner's editors "could not stomach it all" and another found it "hard sledding." Old Charles Scribner himself was skeptical: "I'm proud of my imprint," he growled. "I cannot publish fiction that is without literary value." A senior editor obediently ratified his judgment, calling the book "frivolous." [14] At the height of the novel's popularity, one of Fitzgerald's best friends, from Princeton, the eminent critic Edmund Wilson, termed it "very immaturely imagined; it is always just verging on the ludicrous. And, finally, it is one of the most illiterate books of any merit ever published It is not only full of bogus ideas and faked literary references but it is full of English words misused with the most reckless abandon." [15]

If the manuscript had not won the support of Max Perkins, a contemporary of Fitzgerald's, that probably would have been the end of F. Scott Fitzgerald: author. But Perkins was captivated by the vitality of the prose and somehow pushed the book to publication.

To top miracle with miracle, the book clicked instantly with the reading public, and Fitzgerald was that year's shining literary star, waking up every morning "with a world of ineffable top loftiness and promise," swept along on "that first wild wind of success and the delicious mist it brings with it."[16]

Of course he felt great. He had taken a shot right in the main vein of that potent blend of aphrodisiacs and amphetamines and steroids, that most wonderful of all legal drugs: success. If its user has some talent, it is a drug that allows him to achieve even more, for it is a powerful stimulant of the confidence gland. "For a shy man," Fitzgerald mused, "it was nice to be somebody except oneself again: to be the 'Author' as one had been 'the Lieutenant.'"[17] Fitzgerald happily gave interviews in which "I told what a great writer 1 was and how I'd achieved the heights," expressing his regret to one interviewer, who had just turned thirty, that he had "let his life slide away without accomplishing anything."[18] And with that confidence that success breeds, the drug's user, sure in his own abilities, may feel within him the drive, the ability, the vision, the need for another rush, and so try to match the accomplishment that gave rise to his success, and not only to match it, but to exceed it.

The same day Fitzgerald received the acceptance letter that changed his life, he added in his note to Perkins: "I'm beginning ... a very ambitious novel called The Demon Lover which will probably take a year. Also I'm writing short stories."[19]

Indeed he was. Riding the rush after *This Side of Paradise* was accepted, Fitzgerald saw short stories everywhere, writing eight of them in the next two months and selling all, in contrast to his dismal record from March to June of that same year when he wrote nineteen stories and "no one bought them, no one even sent personal letters."[20] His ninth story was purchased "by the same magazine that had rejected it four months before."[21] On November 1, he sold his first story to *The Saturday Evening Post,* and three months later he had sold the *Post* six more. "I had been an amateur before; in October, when I strolled with a girl among the stones of a southern graveyard, I was a professional and my enchantment with certain things that she felt and said was already paced by an anxiety to set them down in a story."[22]

Was it not this wonder drug that allowed Scott Fitzgerald to move beyond the youthful meanderings of *This Side of Paradise* to the clear professionalism of *The Great Gatsby* published five years later? "I feel I have an enormous power in me now, more than I've ever had," Fitzgerald wrote to Perkins in 1924.[23] His early success gave him the head of steam to keep on writing and perfecting his art. "I want to be one of the greatest writers who ever lived," he confided to Edmund Wilson.[24]

So what was the trouble with all this?

The trouble was that everyone — every reader, every writer, every would-be writer, even Scott Fitzgerald himself — analyzed all the evidence, every clue, and assumed the mystery of what makes a book popular had been solved. Case closed. Everyone mixed up this hole-in-one miracle, the wildly improbable success of *This Side of Paradise* — a novel written in two months, a contract in hand in two weeks, publication five months later, and, although he did not live happily ever after, the young Fitzgerald did find some fame and fortune and the hand of the girl he loved — everyone mixed all this up with the real world of publishing. So compelling is his story, and so strongly do we want to believe in it, that it still shines brightly on the dusty shelf of exhibits, a false clue misleading each generation of authors and publishers struggling to solve the mystery of what makes a book sell.

Whenever the F. Scott Fitzgerald exhibit is re-examined, another musty file should be dusted off — the folder containing the story of one of his contemporaries, a woman one year older than Scott. This woman's novel was a main selection of the Book-of-the-Month Club and achieved that which Fitzgerald could only dream about all his life: It was a runaway best-seller, firmly entrenched for months on the *New York Times Best Sellers* list. That one book sold more hard-cover copies than would all of Fitzgerald's novels combined during his lifetime. Had he been around to witness it, Scott would surely have envied the media blitz that this book attracted — front page of the *New York Times* with a three-column headline and a two-column photograph of its author, coverage on all the major television networks and in all the news magazines, *60 Minutes*, the works.

Now, there was a significant difference between these two authors. While success came to Fitzgerald at twenty-three, Helen Hooven Santmyer's novel, ...*And Ladies of the Club*, became a best-seller when she was eighty-eight, blind in one eye with a cataract in the other, her eighty-pound body wracked by arthritis and emphysema, confined to her wheelchair in her book-filled room at Hospitality Home East, a nursing home in her hometown of Xenia, Ohio. Miss Santmyer's joy, naturally, was somewhat more subdued than that of the young Fitzgerald running up and down the streets of St. Paul, stopping cars to tell his friends the good news. "All this publicity was fun for a while," said the old lady, "but sometimes I wish it would go away. It gets very tiresome."[25] She celebrated her book's success by getting her first permanent wave.

Santmyer had graduated from Wellesley a year before Fitzgerald graduated from Princeton. She received a bachelor of letters degree from Oxford and began working as a secretary to the editor at Scribner's magazine. The two novels she wrote in the 1920s, in her twenties, were dropped down that bottomless literary well where lost books fall without even delivering the satisfaction of a ker-plunk when they hit the water.

As an energized Scott and Zelda were partying around Europe, living happily in their dream world which "every day in every way grew better and better," [26] that fleeting moment, as Fitzgerald described it, "when the fulfilled future and the wistful past were mingled in a single gorgeous moment — when life was literally a dream,"[27] Miss Santmyer became the dean of women at Cedarville College in Ohio and later a reference librarian, working in her spare moments on what would become . . . *And Ladies of the Club*, her sixty-four-year history of a women's literary club in a small town in Ohio. Completed when she was young, her book did not find a publisher until 1982, when Ohio State University Press brought out a $35 edition of the massive novel, which sold a grand total of 1,300 copies. One day an Ohio woman heard a reader tell a fellow library patron that the novel she was returning was the best she had ever read. Intrigued, the lady read it and agreed, sending it on to her son, a Los Angeles film director, who also agreed and showed it to an industry friend, who agreed and sent it to his agent, who brought it to Putnam's, which purchased it for $50,000, published it, and sold 410,000 copies.

The history of . . . *And Ladies of the Club* is a pretty frightening story — waiting until you're eighty-eight for the world to discover — by pure chance — that what you had written really was pretty good after all. How about now climbing the creaking steps to the attic of the house of publishing to see what else may befall a book?

What's that? That noise in the dark at the top of the steps? Too late — there's no turning back now. Here it is, the scary story of John Kennedy Toole, who at the age of twenty-five, completed his first novel, which he titled *A Confederacy of Dunces*. It was a book into which he had poured himself and his ambition and his talent; a book, his Book, that became for him the reason for life. Seven years later, he still had not been able to find a publisher willing to take it on, and, at the age of thirty-two, he was found asphyxiated in his car.

Toole's mother, Thelma, a retired teacher of the dramatic arts, had faith in her son's book from the start. "I've been reading since I was a little girl and I knew John's book was good," she said. "When he came back from the Army he gave it to me and I finished it the next night. It was great, I told him."[28] After his death, his mother began her crusade, taking her dog-eared, smudged carbon copy of the manuscript from publisher to publisher. Each of the publishing houses to which she submitted the manuscript turned it down. For seven years, Mrs. Toole sent the tattered manuscript off to publishers and waited. And eight times, she saw it come back. "Every time it came back, I died a little."[29]

Somehow Mrs. Toole, hurrying in with her walker, buttonholed novelist Walker Percy, who was teaching a seminar at Loyola University near Mrs. Toole's home, and begged him to read the manuscript. Rather reluctantly, he agreed.

Percy took one look at the "badly smeared, scarcely readable carbon"[30] of the manuscript and regretted that he ever had promised Mrs. Toole he would read it. Nevertheless, he waded in and read on. "And on. First with the sinking feeling that it was not bad enough to quit, then with a prickle of interest, then a growing excitement, and finally an incredulity: surely it was not possible that it was so good." [31] Percy arranged its publication in 1980 by Louisiana State University Press when his own publisher — Farrar, Straus and Giroux — rejected it. Louisiana State University Press? Yes. Even the press was astounded. "The book is absolutely marvelous," the editor there wrote to Percy, "but why is it still in manuscript? Hasn't anyone else seen it?"[32]

There were still doubts, even with this editor. "It didn't take long to recognize that there was something of quality here although I admit I felt it was a book that would only have regional appeal. Frankly, I was astonished at the national response."[33] Within a month of publication, the national media were lavishing praise on *A Confederacy of Dunces*, it was into its fourth printing, the Book-of-the-Month Club had purchased it, and Louisiana State University Press (which printed up shopping bags proclaiming "LSU Press brings home the bacon") had sold the paperback, foreign and film rights. The paperback sold a robust 750,000 copies. And on April 13, 1981, Mrs. Toole was notified that her late son had won the 1980 Pulitzer Prize for fiction. If Walker Percy had not agreed to read it, she sighed, "I could not have gone on after being rejected by eight publishers. I was wrecked!"[34]

The title John Kennedy Toole had chosen for his novel became a particularly apt description of the fifteen year story of its publication: Jonathan Swift's dictum that: "When a true genius appears in the world, you may know him by this sign, that the dunces are all in confederacy against him."

"Why, the question nags, why on earth was it not published till now?" asked the New York Times in a review of the book. "Are we to believe that for a period of 15 years a confederacy of publishing dunces rejected the manuscript of a comic genius?"[35]

Well, that's a good question. Where now are those myopic editors who had been lurking in the haunted attic, who read or skimmed the manuscript, or said they did, and breezily scrawled their verdict on one of those rejection letters? Can't you just see them? "I am afraid that . . ." Not our cup of tea." "No market." "Maybe a short magazine piece."

"It isn't about anything. It could be improved, but it wouldn't sell," read the actual rejection letter from Simon & Schuster which Mrs. Toole said was written by "a creature . . . Not a man. Not a human being. I hope I never meet him ..."[36] "You can't stand the heartache of the correspondence," said Mrs. Toole about her son's letters back and forth to publishers.[37]

To round out the horror tales of Helen Hooven Santmyer and John Kennedy Toole, one more exhibit must be examined, just one more; and that, of course, is the rest of the file on F. Scott Fitzgerald, whose ghost haunts every American writer's imagination.

Later in his life, Scott Fitzgerald recalled a day soon after the publication of *This Side of Paradise* and his marriage to Zelda, "riding in a taxi one afternoon between very tall buildings under a mauve and rosy sky; I began to bawl because I had everything I wanted and knew I would never be so happy again."[38] He described this period of bliss, of euphoria, that he felt after the publication and success of his first novel as "a short and precious time — for when the mist rises in a few weeks, or a few months, one finds that the very best is over."[39] It certainly was for him. Life never again would be so good, and he never again would know the public's adoration, or the financial rewards, he assumed would be his.

Fitzgerald was sure that his third novel, *The Great Gatsby,* published in 1925 when its author had achieved the ripe old age of twenty-nine, was special. "My book has something extraordinary about it. I want to be extravagantly admired again."[40] A few weeks before publication, he was hopeful that it would sell 75,000 copies. But the book was a disappointment to its author, selling only about 20,000 copies, just enough to cover Fitzgerald's advance. In 1929, Fitzgerald earned $27,000 for eight short stories published in the *Saturday Evening Post,* but only $31.77 in royalties from his books, including $5.10 for *The Great Gatsby.*

Sales of his next book, *Tender is the Night,* were even worse, about 10,000, in a year when Hervey *Allen's Anthony Adverse* sold over one million copies. "Alas," Fitzgerald sighed in a letter to Perkins, "I may again have written a novel for novelists with little chance of its lining anybody's pockets with gold."[41]

"Cards began falling for us much too early," Scott wrote to Zelda as he looked back on his failure to achieve that early promise of success that seemed to be his.[42] His books weren't selling. His life had become a week-by-week battle to scrape together enough money to exist. "My birthday is two-column front page news as if I were 80 instead of 40 — and I sit worrying about next week's $35.00 hotel bill!"[43] How much worse could it get? Let's see. He spoke to the dean of Princeton about giving a series of lectures on fiction at the university. No thank you, Dean Gaus replied; why don't you try one of the eating clubs?

Here was an author who had written the best books that he could write, books he was certain were very good indeed; books that today are recognized as great, as classics. Yet these books were all but ignored when published. Is it any wonder this author would suffer a breakdown at thirty-nine?

Published after Fitzgerald's death in 1940 at the age of forty-four, *The Last Tycoon* was critically praised, but that was all. "I hope the book will sell," Zelda wrote to Max Perkins, "at least enough to repay your interest."[44] It didn't. It sold 3,268 copies that year.

It's always been assumed that Fitzgerald's books were out of print when he died. Fitzgerald was afraid this would happen; he had told Max Perkins how odd it would be when his daughter "assures her friends I was an author and finds that no book is procurable."[45] As Charles Scribner III noted, "The truth is sadder: they were all in stock at our warehouse and listed in the catalogue, but there were no orders."[46]

It was only after Fitzgerald's friend, Edmund Wilson, put together some of Scott's miscellaneous writings in a volume which he titled *The Crack-Up* — a volume, by the way, which was turned down by every major New York publisher before it was brought out by New Directions in 1945 — that a Fitzgerald revival began and the importance of his writing began to be recognized. Today, Fitzgerald's place as one of the American masters is secure. Today, *The Crack-Up* is still in print. Today, biographies of Scott, of Zelda, of their friends, sell more copies than his own books did in his lifetime. Today, all his books are in print and all continue to sell. And sell, and sell. In 1990, Charles Scribner, Jr., remarked that year after year *The Great Gatsby* "has had the biggest sales of any Scribner's book; in fact, it is the best-selling book in the history of our company."[47]

The question of course is why Fitzgerald's books didn't receive the recognition and the sales they deserved during his lifetime. He was, after all, a very visible author, an author in the public eye right from the publication of *This Side of Paradise* when he was twenty-three years old. What had happened? And what if Edmund Wilson hadn't published *The Crack-Up* and started a Fitzgerald revival? Would his novels have been lost forever?

Publishing is a mysterious business. It is a business that tries desperately to find, among the thousands of books coming to market annually, those two hundred or so which will be the year's best-sellers; yet it does little, if anything, to encourage the development of the authors who will write those books. In fact, it does quite a bit to discourage them. It is an industry littered with what Anthony Trollope called "that huge pile of futile literature, the building up of which has broken so many hearts,"[48] an industry littered with ruined books and shattered dreams, of authors as disillusioned, embittered, as frustrated as the author who, in 1979, rented an airplane and buzzed the mid- Manhattan offices of his publisher, Harcourt Brace Jovanovich.

The editor at Simon & Schuster who John Kennedy Toole's mother referred to as "a creature. . .Not a man. Not a human being," was Robert Gottlieb, who would become one of the most famous editors of the second half of the twentieth century. Fifty years after he received the draft of *A Confederacy of Dunces*, Gottlieb published his memoirs, and recounted how he had "several years of back and forth" with Toole about his manuscript. In reviewing their correspondence, Gottlieb wrote: "I'm surprised . . . at how likeable and rational, how wiling he appears in it . . . As time passed, though, I began to sense that his mind, or psyche, was beginning to fray, and after he made an ill-considered (and unannounced) visit to our office, creating an irrational and unnerving scene, I decided that I had to end our affair."[49]

"Several years back and forth"? "As time passed"? Did this distinguished editor not perceive how jerking an author who undoubtedly
knew his manuscript was good — it would, after all, win the Pulitzer
Prize after Toole's death — might lead to a fraying of "his mind, or
psyche"? And that if his editorial sense of time was so different from
an author's, then armed security guards in the reception area of the
publishing house might not be such a bad idea in case of "ill considered" or, heaven forbid, "unannounced" visits to the office?

Does a good book eventually, ultimately, inevitably, find a publisher and then an audience?

Ernest Hemingway almost didn't make it. Frustrated and discouraged by the repeated delays in the publication of his first book,
In Our Time, twenty-five-year-old Hemingway wrote to Ezra Pound:
"Now we haven't got any money anymore I am going to have to quit
writing and I never will have a book published. I feel cheerful as hell
. . . Fuck literature."[50] It took the collective pulling and pushing and
persuasion of Pound, Scott Fitzgerald and Gertrude Stein to break
him into print.

Tennessee Williams almost didn't make it. "Before the success of
Menagerie I'd reached the very, very bottom. I would have died without the money. I couldn't have gone on any further, baby, without
money, when suddenly, providentially, *The Glass Menagerie* made it
when I was thirty- four."[51]

Theodore Dreiser almost didn't make it. As E.L. Doctorow has
explained it:

Dreiser wrote this magnificent novel *[Sister Carrie]*.
It was published in 1900; it was then and is still the best first
novel ever written by an American. It's an amazing work
The book was a magnificent achievement but the publisher, Doubleday, didn't like it, they were afraid of it. So they
buried it. And naturally it did nothing; I think it sold four

copies. I would go crazy too in that situation… [He] ended up in a sanitarium in Westchester, in White Plains."[52]

Hemingway. Williams. Dreiser. Just three examples of famous authors who did find a publisher, but who came very close to falling into the abyss.

The whole mysterious business of publishing calls forth such doubts that when we see an author who does make it, we can only wonder: is that proof that the system works? Or are there scores of other accomplished writers out there who never got the necessary lucky break?

Getting published is just the first break from Lady Luck. Once the book is in print, another big break is needed to get it to find its audience, to sell.

Why are certain books popular? No one seems to know. The secrets of what makes a book a best-seller are out of sight behind false panels, down hidden staircases, up in dusty attics, under haunted bridges. "Predicting which those will be is almost as much a game of chance as roulette," Brigitte Weeks, the former editor-in-chief of the Book-of-the-Month Club, has said.[53] Robert Loomis, an editor with Random House for over thirty-five years who has an enviable list of best-sellers to his credit, admitted that he had never been able to unravel the secret of best-seller success.[54]

It doesn't take much sleuthing to discover that the mystery of what makes a book sell has the publishing industry baffled. Evidence of bafflement is in plain sight.

Consider Henry Roth's *Call It Sleep*, published in 1934 to mixed reviews. The book quickly disappeared, and Roth gave up writing and became a manual laborer, psychiatric hospital attendant, factory worker. Thirty years later, *Call It Sleep* was reissued as a paperback; Irving Howe on the front page of the *New York Times Book Review* hailed it as an American classic, and the paperback went on to sell more than one million copies.

Look at Christina Stead's *The Man Who Loved Children*. In 1940 Simon & Schuster brought it out to mediocre reviews and modest sales, then let it go out of print. In 1965 the book was republished by Holt, Rinehart and Winston to great reviews and great sales.

How about the twenty publishers who turned down Richard Bach's *Jonathan Livingston Seagull*, the twenty-six who rejected Irving Stone's *Lust for Life*, the twenty-seven who said no thank you to Dr. Seuss's *And to Think That I Saw It on Mulberry Street*, the twenty- eight who rejected John Grisham's *A Time to Kill*, the forty who passed on the opportunity to publish Nabokov's *Lolita*?

Even when books are accepted for publication, their publishers often have no idea of their worth. How about the $3,000 advance to Jacqueline Susann for *Valley of the Dolls*, the $5,000 advance to Tom Clancy for *The Hunt for Red October*, the $3,000 advance to Stephen King for *Carrie*? These publishers had not the vaguest notion of the mega-hits they had just purchased.

How about a book just like the latest best-seller? Just when publishers think they have solved the mystery of what makes a best-selling book, just when they have begun to distribute their advances accordingly to the authors of "sure" hits, along comes something that blows all their theories out of the water. How about *The Name of the Rose*, written by an Italian professor, an intricately plotted novel set in fourteenth century Europe, interspersed with Latin passages? Harcourt Brace Jovanovich had bought the book for a modest $4,000. The book sold over a million copies and the paperback rights were sold to Warner Books for $550,000. And, for heaven's sake, how about *A Brief History of Time* by British physicist Stephen Hawking, an all but impenetrable guide to astrophysics and the nature of time and the universe, which graced the *New York Times Best Sellers* list for over two years, with more than four months at the highest spot?

Samuel Butler said that, "There are some things which it is madness not to try to know but which it is almost as much madness to try to know. Sometimes publishers, hoping to buy the Holy Ghost with a price, fee a man to read for them and advise them. This is but as the vain tossing of insomnia. God will not have any human being know what will sell."[55]

How can this be? How can the formula of what makes a book sell so long remain a mystery? Season after season? Decade after decade?

Maybe God's not telling, but anyone involved with writing and publishing long enough may uncover at least a few clues as to what makes books sell. If we sift through some of the shop talk of authors, publishers, editors and agents, in interviews, diaries, notebooks, letters, journals, memoirs and biographies, we find evidence — sometimes circumstantial, but evidence nonetheless — a clue here, a confession there.

Well, if that's true, then what the heck happened to poor Scott Fitzgerald? Why wasn't *The Great Gatsby* the hit it should have been? It's a cold case, but can we follow any clues and do a post mortem?

Certainly the novel itself, the story, has more than stood the test of time. Its position as a classic, a masterpiece, is unassailable. So the cause of its death when first published wasn't a lethal blow.

Fitzgerald himself was concerned about the title. Titles certainly didn't come easily to him. In draft form, he was calling his first novel *The Romantic Egotist*, a title with which he tinkered that fateful summer as he slaved away in St. Paul for the hand of the girl he loved, coming up with *The Education of a Personage*, and then, late in the summer — he got it and he knew it — *This Side of Paradise*, an evocative, haunting title that did the trick for a book coming out right after World War I, just at the beginning of the Roaring Twenties.

The Great Gatsby was another story. On October 27, 1924, Fitzgerald sent to Max Perkins the manuscript of this novel, which he alternately was calling *Trimalchio in West Egg* or *The Great Gatsby*. In his covering letter, the noted. "I have an alternative title: *Gold-hatted Gatsby*.[56] A week later, in his next letter, he was floundering: "I have not decided to stick to the title I put on the book, *Trimalchio in West Egg*. The only other titles that seem to fit it are *Trimalchio* and *On the Road to West Egg*, I had two others, *Gold- hatted Gatsby* and *The High-bouncing Lover*, but they seem too slight. A month later, he was still mulling over titles, including *Among Ash Heaps and Millionaires* and still *Trimalchio in West Egg*. "Maybe simply *Trimalchio* or *Gatsby*."[57] On January 24, 1925, in a p.s. to a letter to Perkins, he noted: "I'm returning the proof of the title page, etc. It's O.K. but my heart tells me I should have named it *Trimalchio*. However, against all advice, I suppose it would have been stupid and stubborn of me. *Trimalchio in West Egg* was only a compromise. *Gatsby* is too much like *Babbitt* and *The Great Gatsby* is weak because there's no emphasis even ironically on his greatness or lack of it. However, let it pass."[58]

What a mistake! Too late he realized it, two weeks before publication date sending off to the Perkins from the isle of Capri a frantic wire: "CRAZY ABOUT TITLE UNDER THE RED WHITE AND BLUE STOP WHAT WOULD DELAY BE?" At that late date, what did he expect an editor to say? Too late, wired Perkins, no doubt breathing a sigh of relief that it was. Fitzgerald was troubled and wrote that "if the book fails commercially it will be . . . [because] "the title is only fair, rather bad than good."[59] Undoubtedly, he attributed *Gatsby's* pitiful sales to its uninspired title, which does seem to miss the mark by a mile. It is a title without melody or music, and, on top of that, not a very apt reflection of the book, as Fitzgerald himself realized. "When books succeed," Simon & Schuster's editor-in-chief, Michael Korda, has said, "it's because their titles are intriguing to us," a sentiment endorsed by many publishers and editors, including Jonathan Segal, a senior editor at Knopf, who noted that any books' "best advertisement is the title."[60]

So maybe it was a weak title which almost derailed Fitzgerald's masterpiece. But as long as we have the exhumed cadaver on the table for the autopsy, how about that hideous dust jacket? *The Great Gatsby's* dust jacket couldn't have helped the cause. The dust jacket for his first novel, *This Side of Paradise*, showed an elegant young couple looking as if they were about to go out on the town for the evening, capturing well a Roaring Twenties image. *The Great Gatsby's* dust jacket is dark, forbidding, featuring the staring eyes of the billboard of Dr. T.J. Eckleburg along the railroad tracks between West Egg and New York City. How much more fitting and seductive might have been an artist's impressionistic rendition of one of Gatsby's parties with his "blue gardens," an orchestra playing "yellow cocktail music," and the "sea- change of faces and voices and color under the constantly changing light," a scene which might have drawn readers to the book "like moths among the whispering and the champagne and the stars."

Every clue of how to publish a book well is hiding in plain sight. Every publisher has uncovered some of them, and some publishers have discovered a lot of them, but few, if any, have tried consistently to apply every one of those principles to each book they publish.

And maybe the real mystery is: why not?

For certainly any book worth publishing is worth publishing well.

AN AUTHOR IN SEARCH OF A CHARACTER — AND HIMSELF:
Gore Vidal Meets Denham Fouts

DENHAM FOUTS WAS BORN IN JACKSONVILLE, FLORIDA, in 1914. By the time of Denny's death in Rome in 1948, the thirty-four year old had more than earned the title Truman Capote bestowed on him of "best-kept boy in the world."

Capote found that "to watch him walk into a room was an experience. He was beyond being good-looking; he was the single most charming-looking person I've ever seen."[1] Gore Vidal said he was "un homme fatal."[2] And his friend Christopher Isherwood called him the most expensive male prostitute in the world. Some of the wealthiest men of the day were instantly smitten, from a shipping tycoon, to the largest land owner in Great Britain, to a prince. His most steadfast benefactor was Peter Watson, the young heir to an enormous English fortune. Watson had sent Denny to the United States at the outbreak of World War II with one of his Picasso oil paintings that is now among the most valuable holdings of the Metropolitan Museum of Art. After the War, Denny returned to Peter's home in Paris. It was there, in April of 1948, that twenty-two year old Gore Vidal came to pay homage to the legend.

In the preceding decade, Eugene Luther Gore Vidal, Jr., had transformed himself into Gore Vidal: young literary lion.

Ten years before, into Gore's rather lonely and unhappy adolescence dominated by a hard drinking, caustic, unpredictable mother he detested, who divorced his father when Gore was ten, (and whose periods, he later wryly commented, had been "more excruciating than those of any other woman in medical history"[3]), into the gray gothic world of St. Albans in Washington, D.C. where his mother sent him as a boarding student, a school where bullies would stampede a student into a locker, lock it, and leave, into this world of adolescent uncertainty and fear had walked a schoolboy god "and the first human happiness that I had ever encountered."[4]

It was winter of 1937, mid-term, when twelve year old Jimmie Trimble arrived at St. Albans. Gore checked out Jimmie's pubic hair in the communal shower — "bright gold curls" — and "as I looked at him, he gave me a big grin and so it began, likeness drawn to likeness, soon to be made whole by desire minus the obligatory pursuit."[5]

Gore's mother was relieved when on occasion her son brought his new friend home for a weekend visit to "Merrywood," Gore's step-father's Georgian mansion set on forty acres above the Potomac River in McLean, Virginia, with tennis court, squash court, pool and woods, surprised that at last her bookish son, who spent all his time reading, had any friend. It was at "Merrywood," on the white tile floor of a bathroom out of view of the butler, that "there we were, belly to belly, in the act of becoming one," where "we simply came together."[6] Presumably also out of view of the butler, Gore and Jimmie roller skated on the driveway at Merrywood "holding each other's cock."[7]

Jimmie would become the golden boy of St. Albans. He was captain of the basketball team, a star of the football team, and a legend of the baseball team, the ace pitcher who strung together a record of no-hitters with his fastballs and curve balls, thrown at such speed that the catcher had to get extra padding for his glove. Jimmie was handsome at twelve, a grown-up, according to Vidal, at fourteen, downright striking at seventeen. There he is in a photograph at seventeen, looking remarkably contemporary in a light-colored boat-neck sweater, no shirt underneath. Is he aware how perfectly that sweater set off his chest and broad shoulders? The thrust of his athlete's neck? The square jaw? The knowing grin, that smile, like Gatsby's, "with a quality of eternal reassurance in it," that smile that, according to another friend, "would just knock the birds out of the trees,"[8] those blue eyes that seemed to look at the humorous side of life, that seemed to intimate that he saw right into everyone? The wavy blonde hair? "Did you ever tell a man that he was *beautiful?*"[9], a shocked Jimmie asked his mother after a girlfriend had used that word to describe him. He was, and to top it off, exuded a definite sexual energy, a masculine magnetism that drew everyone into his world. He was like Phineas in John Knowles' *A Separate Peace*, with no one immune from his pull. A retired English master from St. Albans, who had taught there when Jimmie Trimble was a student, recalled that Jimmie "moved through the Lane Johnston halls briskly, but when he idled along, he had a generous roll of the hips — the flexible hips of the athlete — that promised, like the Anglican definition of faith — 'the substance of things hoped for, the evidence of things unseen.' But I was too much the unsure 27 year-old master to do more than cast my eyes demurely down, probably not too far down, as he passed by."[10] Clearly when Jimmie walked by, there were masters and students, male and female admirers, silently staring.

Late Spring, 1939. Before leaving for a school trip to France, Gore remembered, "Jimmie and I made love in the woods above the roaring river. I remember his almost-mature body with the squared bony shoulders and rosy skin against bright green. ... After sex, we swam against the swift, deadly current of the forbidden Potomac River, swam among rocks and driftwood to a special large gray-brown glacial rock, where we lay, side by side. We're going to go on doing this for the rest of our lives, I remember thinking, tempting — no, driving — fate to break us in two. ... Every now and then, in idle moments, I start to hear snatches of the conversation of those two boys on the rock that afternoon," on that "cloudless sunny day when Europe was ahead of me and all I cared for beside me."[11]

After the summer, Gore was sent to Los Alamos Ranch School in New Mexico, and the following year to Exeter in New Hampshire, while Jimmie stayed at St. Albans.

The next time, and the last time, Gore saw Jimmie was during the 1942 Christmas season when the two met at the holiday dance of Mrs. Shippen's Dancing School. "We had last seen each other as fourteen year-old boys. Now we were seventeen year-old men. Would we take up where we had left off in the Spring of 1939 on a May day, in the woods above the Potomac River?"[12] It was an awkward reunion when they spotted each other in their tuxedos in the ballroom with their dates. Gore had known Rosalind for several years, and the two just had announced that they would marry after Gore graduated from Exeter in June, before his enlistment in the Army in July. Gore told Jimmie of his marriage plans. "You're crazy," Jimmie said, as the two of them left their dates and walked downstairs to the men's room. ." . . [O]ur bodies still fitted perfectly together, as we promptly discovered inside one of the cubicles, standing up, belly to belly, talking of girls and marriage and coming simultaneously."[13]

As soon as he turned eighteen Jimmie enlisted in the Marine Corps. He and his girlfriend, Christine White, voted the "prettiest blonde" at her school, agreed to marry when Jimmie returned from service. In July of 1944, Trimble joined the Third Marine Division in the South Pacific and Vidal enlisted in the Army and found himself on a ship in the Aleutians.

After serving for several months on Guam where he was the star pitcher for the his Marine Division's baseball team, Trimble volunteered to join a scouting platoon for the landing on Iwo Jima. The stark statistics bespeak the horror of those bloody days. Twenty-two thousand Japanese defended the four mile island. It would take the American forces over a month to control the island at a cost of seven thousand dead and more than twenty thousand wounded, with all but one thousand Japanese soldiers dead.

Eight days after the first landing, Jimmie joined a reconnaissance team trying to pinpoint the location of rocket sites so that artillery could be called in to take them out. In a midnight attack on his team's fox hole, a Japanese soldier with a mine strapped to him jumped in and wrapped himself around Jimmie, blowing both of them to death.

That Spring, the Marine's Third Division baseball field on Guam was officially dedicated as Trimble Field, a story reported in all the Washington, D.C. newspapers. There was a memorial service held in the Washington Cathedral where Jimmie lay in state. "I can't think of how a nineteen year-old Marine private would merit a 'state' burial," Vidal wondered years later, "but on the other hand, he was much loved by Washington sports fans."[14]

As for Gore Vidal, from that day he last saw him "and left Jimmie to time and chance,"[15] his world never again was the same. He would think of him the rest of his life. Hanging on the wall beside his bed was a life-size reproduction of an oil portrait of Jimmie as a teenager. Now and then, Jimmie would appear to him in visions, as "completely present, as he had been in the bedroom of Merrywood": Jimmie "opened his blue eyes and smiled and yawned and put his hand alongside my neck."[16] And "for years, whenever I was in a numinous place like Delphi or Delos, I would address the night: Jimmie, are you anywhere? And almost always the wind would rise."[17] Late in his life, Vidal bought a small plot in Rock Creek Park Cemetery in Washington, D.C., just a few yards from where Jimmie Trimble lay in the shade of a copper beech.

Looking back from the vantage point of his seventh decade, Vidal realized that when he was with Jimmie Trimble, he was whole "for what proved to be the last time . . . I not only never again encountered the other half, but by the time I was twenty-five, I had given up all pursuit, settling for a thousand brief anonymous adhesions Quite enough, I think if the real thing has happened."[18]

Vidal's emergence as a prominent author had been all but instantaneous. He graduated from Exeter in June of 1943, entered the Enlisted Reserve Corps of the Army the next month, became the first mate of an army supply ship in the Aleutians, and on his night watches began drafting in pencil in an accounts book his first novel. He completed his book nine months later. *Williwaw* —an Eskimo term for the violent storms that bore down on the Bering Sea — was based on his own military experience, published in 1946 by Dutton, and hailed as one of the first war novels, and by a nineteen year-old author, no less. Vidal immediately assumed a place among those perceived as the next generation of American literary lions.

"With the finishing of this book, my life as a writer began."[19] Books tumbled out of him. The next year, he published *In a Yellow Wood*, a coming-of-age novel in which the main character had to choose between a predictable life and an unconventional life style, perhaps reflecting the tensions Vidal was feeling between the pull of a political life — following in the footsteps of his grandfather, Senator Thomas Gore — or a more bohemian, literary life; perhaps reflecting the tensions he was feeling between a married life or what was then the hidden life of someone with a same sex orientation: Rosalind versus Jimmie. Whatever its origins, it was a minor book Vidal later in his life would call his "worst novel."[20]

His next more than made up for this lackluster performance. Published less than a year later, on January 10, 1948, *The City and the Pillar* was dedicated "For the memory of J.T.," and was, as Vidal described it, a novel in which he described what might have happened had he and Jimmie met again after the War. Vidal knew he was moving into uncharted, dangerous territory with this book. "I knew that my description of the love affair between two normal all-American boys of the sort that I had spent three years with in the wartime army would challenge every superstition about sex in my native land."[21] Indeed, after he read the new novel, Orville Prescott, the influential book reviewer for the *New York Times*, told Vidal's editor that he would never again read, much less review, a book by Vidal. *The Times* refused to advertise it, as did all major newspapers and magazines. "In freedom's land," Vidal wrote years later in describing the shock caused by his new novel, "what ought not to be is not and must be blacked out."[22] But within two weeks of publication, *The City and the Pillar* was riding the *New York Times* Best-Sellers list along with Truman Capote's *Other Voices, Other Rooms* and Norman Mailer's *The Naked and the Dead*, and a triumphant twenty-two year old Vidal was off to Rome. There, at a dinner party in February, he met and befriended the famed thirty-seven year old playwright, Tennessee Williams, whose *A Streetcar Named Desire* was then a national sensation and a year later would win a Pulitzer Prize. The two traveled around Italy in an old Jeep Tennessee had bought, and Gore remembered never in his life laughing so much with anyone.

From Rome, the two friends in April drove to Paris where "there were Bellow and Mailer and Capote and Baldwin and Bowles, while Tennessee and I shared a floor of the small Hotel de L'Universite."[23]

This amazing assemblage of young authors was soon augmented by the arrival of Christopher Isherwood, who, with his lover, Bill Caskey, landed at LeHavre on April 22. They immediately made their way to Paris, past the many reminders of the War — "small military graveyards, smashed houses, provisional half-rebuilt bridges over which the train moved cautiously" — straight to Peter Watson's apartment on the Rue du Bac to see Denny Fouts who had stayed with Isherwood in California during the War.[24]

It was a Saturday evening, April 24, 1948. Christopher recorded his impressions of Denny in his diary:

> It is a huge shabby place with traces of the splendor of his pre-1939 period, in which he leads a nocturnal Proustian life with the tattered curtains always drawn. He lies most

of the day in bed, with Trotsky [his dog] and the [opium] pipe at his side, reading and dozing, often eating nothing but a plate of cooked cereal. When he can't afford opium, he drinks a kind of tea made of the dross, which gives him stomach cramps. He is as pale as a corpse, but quite unchanged, slim as ever, and a sort of waxen beauty. He did not seem at all vague or stupefied, . . . and he welcomed us both warmly.[25]

The next day, Christopher and Bill were sitting in the Café des Deux Magots when Gore Vidal walked by, recognized Isherwood and stopped to introduce himself. Earlier in the year, Vidal had sent him an advance copy of *The City and the Pillar* seeking an endorsement, and the famed author had praised it. When he sat down to talk, Gore asked Christopher advice on how to manage his writing career, and the two struck up a friendship that would last for years, each appreciating the other's sense of humor. (Both later admitted that in this first encounter, each felt the other was flirting, but neither made the first move, then or ever).

The next evening and the next, Isherwood, Caskey and Vidal dined together. It was the second evening that this group joined up with John Lehmann, Isherwood's publisher; through Isherwood's introduction, Vidal engaged Lehmann as his English publisher. As Vidal described him, he had "a tiger's grin, liked to call people Ducky" and "sexually, it was his pleasure to beat working-class boys; otherwise, he lived a life of perfect domestic virtue. ..."[26]

After dinner, the friends took Vidal to Peter Watson's home at 44 Rue du Bac to visit Denny, into his room with the great bed and the "magnificent Tchelitchev painting hanging over it."[27]

Vidal noted that "Denham's legendary beauty was not visible to me."[28] This may have been because Denny was the anti-Jimmie. If Jimmie was the all-American boy next door, then Denny was a walking orgasm. Gore saw Denny as "very pale, with dark lank Indian hair and blank dark eyes, usually half shut: . . . He was slender and boyish, with a markedly asymmetrical face."[29]

Gore sat on the side of Denny's bed with John Lehmann, with Trotsky — Denny's black sheepdog — sprawled on the other side. Denny began his ritualistic ceremony of preparing his opium pipe, "inhaled deeply and exhaled slowly blue medicinal-smelling smoke."[30] Trotsky greedily inhaled the smoke.

"Here," he said to Gore, handing him the long opium pipe.

Gore protested that he couldn't even inhale cigarette smoke, but, good guest that he was, gave it a try, had a "coughing fit" and was "deathly ill."[31] Other than politely offering his visitors a chance to smoke, Denny never pressed anyone to keep trying. As Isherwood remembered the evening, "he let us all take puffs at the pipe, scolding us for our awkwardness and saying we should never make real smokers. It tasted like incense and had no apparent effect whatsoever."[32] As the others watched, Denny continued his ritual, his eyes half shut, then closed, and then, after a while, began to speak, his lulling voice of midnight now a run-on jumble of a monologue of people and places and thoughts:

"Cyril [Connolly] was just here. His first trip to Paris since the war. Peter [Watson] and I took him to a restaurant down the street where he ordered a huge lunch — he's very fat and greedy, you know — and he ate it all up very fast and then he ordered a second lunch and ate that, too. Then he fainted. The waiters carried him back here and put him over there on the floor. I want to meet Truman Capote. I have his picture here."[33]

The *Life* magazine with the famous photograph of the young Capote, drilling the camera with smoldering eyes, rested under one of Denny's opium pipes. Gore told Denny he was sure they would get along.

Denny continued: "I've just had a telegram from Prince Paul [of Greece] — only he's King Paul now. We lived together — well, traveled a lot together before the war, but then he had to get married to Frederika and so we stopped seeing each other because I was living in Santa Monica by then anyway and working in that bookshop and seeing Chris [Isherwood] and Gerald [Heard]. "[34]

Fascinated by what he was hearing, Gore was skeptical. Were all the names, all these stories, a result of the opium haze? As he soon learned, Denham never fabricated a story.

It was a few days later, on April 29, when the group met Denny for cocktails at the Ritz. Isherwood described Denny as looking like "Dorian Gray emerging from the tomb — death-pale and very slim in his dark elegant suit, with black hat and umbrella. He looks like the Necropolitan ambassador."[35] After he sat down, Denny asked Bill Caskey to take some money and get a package of opium from a "connection" who was waiting outside the restaurant. Isherwood thought this request outrageous and refused to let Caskey go, afraid the police could be watching the pusher and that Caskey would be arrested. He felt that Denny's suggestion "was an entirely characteristic act of aggression."[36] (After Christopher left Paris at the end of April, Denny sent him a letter: "I hope you and Bill will go on being happy as you seem to be." Isherwood noted that "Denny obviously didn't hope it.")[37]

Isherwood found that Denny seemed to be quite himself, not in the least "depressed or debauched or down-at-hell." But his stomach cramps may have been acting up that evening for he merely picked at the caviar and watched the others eat "with an air of controlled distaste, as though our addiction to solid food were a far more squalid vice than his. Now and then, his manner became a trifle vague, but his wit was as sharp as ever."[38]

Gore had read in that day's paper that King Paul had pneumonia, and as the evening wore down, he mentioned this to Denny.

"I must send him a telegram," Denny said, and together, Gore and Denny located on St. Germain a Western Union office still open where Denny sent the telegram.

The next day, Denny showed Gore the reply telegram he received from the King:

"Darling Denham, so wonderful to hear from you. Why haven't I heard from you before? Much exaggerated about my illness . . . Love, Paul."[39]

It was then that Gore realized all of Denny's stories were true.

Vidal began visiting Denny regularly. (Isherwood wrote in his memoirs that "Denny treats Gore with the slightly sarcastic tolerance of an elder uncle."[40]) "At sundown," Vidal recalled, "like Dracula, Denham would appear in the streets leading his dog down St.-Germain-des-Pres."[41]

Here, certainly, was a character in search of an author, and Vidal, consciously or not, filed in his memory-bank his encounters with Denny. It was not long, just two years, before Denny first appeared in his fiction.

It was the summer of 1950 when he was twenty-four. Vidal had just bought "Edgewater," a run-down Greek revival mansion on the Hudson River in Dutchess County, New York, ninety miles from New York City.

The first book he wrote in the soaring twenty-six foot high octagonal library at "Edgewater," looking out over the Hudson River and Catskill Mountains, was *The Judgement of Paris*, a book he always regarded as one of his favorites and sometimes called his best book, "the novel in which I found my own voice."[42] This picaresque novel centers on the wanderings of Philip Warren, a twenty-eight year old American, a graduate of Harvard Law School, who travels around

Italy, France and Egypt after the Second World War, just as Vidal visited Rome, Paris and Cairo in 1948 and 1949. One of the characters Philip encounters in Paris is Jim. Vidal later confirmed that this Jim was the same Jim Willard from *The City and the Pillar*, who was Jimmie Trimble. "High romantics who fall from the heights make very good drug addicts. I suppose, unconsciously, I was grafting onto him . . . some characteristics of a marvelous southern whore named Denham Fouts."[43]

How close to the mark was Vidal's portrayal of Denny as Jim in *The Judgement of Paris*? Who better to assess his accuracy than Denny's younger friend and lover, the artist, Michael Wishart, who characterized as "brilliant" Vidal's vignette of Denham, with Denny appearing in the novel "very much in character."[44] As Vidal sat on the side of Denny's bed, as he dined with him, the young author was exploring the thoughts of so strange a character, gathering material, and the essence of their conversations found their way into this novel.

In *The Judgment of Paris*, Philip Warren when in Paris meets Jim, with his "low southern voice" and "slow engaging smile," Jim, dressed "like a conservative schoolboy in dark grey trousers and a sports coat," just as Denny dressed. Vidal has given this character "golden hair and dark blue eyes," fusing Jimmie Trimble's physical characteristics onto Denny. Jim invites Philip to join him the next evening at an outdoor café. They meet, and in a coming storm, Jim takes Philip to his apartment where the bedroom is very much like Denny's with "a large carved bed of dark wood with four posters" in the center of the room and on the mantle "unframed drawings of Tchelichew and Picaso."

Gathering through their conversation the nature of Jim's profession, Philip, curious, begins inquiring about his lifestyle.

As they talk and drink more Pernod, Jim asks Philip if he likes boys. When Philip answers no, and, upon the next question — "not even once, in school?" — responds no, Jim then inquires "would you like to?", to which Philip responds no, that he's too old to change his habits, and upon further pressing — "you wouldn't like to try?" — declines again the invitation.

The rain had stopped and the two go across the street for dinner. "'They got wonderful snails across the street,' Jim said.

'I don't like snails.'

'Have you ever tried any?'

'No.'

'Well, how do you know?' They both laughed."[45]

Denny's role in *The Judgment of Paris* is of a minor, secondary character, one of the unusual specimens the narrator meets in his youthful wanderings. It is in one Vidal's early short stories that a character based on Denham Fouts plays a more pivotal role.

In his memoirs published in 1995, Vidal reveals that he never kept a diary or journal, no record of his days other than "thirteen green pages of notes from 1961 and a diary kept for a month or two in 1948."[46] The notes from 1961 concerned his encounters with President John F. Kennedy in his first year in office, a time when Vidal, who had unsuccessfully run for Congress the year before, still harbored political ambitions, in short, encounters he realized at the time were of special interest and importance. Why would he keep a diary for several months in 1948, the only other time in a very active life during which he kept contemporaneous notes of daily events? Their significance deepens because these were the *only* pages he would not give to his biographers and are, in fact, the *only* pages among all of his papers given to the University of Wisconsin, and then transferred to Harvard, to be sealed until fifty years "after my death or the Second Coming, whichever comes first."[47] Certainly this year, 1948, was, in Vidal's estimation, an "annus mirabilis" as he called it — a bestseller to his credit, his emergence as a personality and celebrity, meeting such famed authors as Tennessee Williams, Christopher Isherwood, Paul Bowles, E.M. Forester, Truman Capote — so it would be natural for him to be recording his experiences and thoughts in a journal. But those are not the sorts of jottings to be kept secreted.

Clues to this mystery may well be found in a short story Vidal wrote at "Edgewater." "Pages From an Abandoned Journal" (certainly the title of the story is intriguing: pages from a diary begun in 1948 and put aside after two months), was published in a collection of his short stories written between 1948 and 1956, titled *A Thirsty Evil*.

The story opens with the narrator's journal entry for April 30, 1948. (It would be interesting if Vidal's diary fragment from 1948 started on that exact date which was, in fact, five days after Vidal met Christopher Isherwood, and three days after he first met Denny Fouts). Peter, an American from Toledo, Ohio (representative, perhaps, of the "normal," of middle America) in Paris working on his doctorate, is engaged to marry Helen when he returns home in the fall.

He is invited to a party at Elliott Magren's apartment. Elliott Magren is the Denham Fouts character in this story, and, appropriately enough, lives on the Rue du Bac, just as Denny lived in Watson's apartment at 44 Rue du Bac. Peter is curious about Elliott, who is "already a legend in Europe,"[48] and so decides to go to the party.

When Peter arrives at ten-thirty that night, he is shown through the four large rooms of the apartment to the last room where Elliott lay on a big bed surrounded by pillows. The room is dimly lit by lamps with red shades, and over the bed hung a painting of a nude man (the famous Tchelitchev oil painting Peter Watson had bought for Denny). He is introduced to Elliott who shook his hand and pulled him next to him on the bed, and asked if he wanted to smoke opium. Peter told him no, he didn't use drugs.

As they sat together on the bed, Elliott lit up his opium pipe and began to talk. "I can't remember a word he said. I was aware, though, that this was probably the most brilliant conversation I'd ever heard. It might have been the setting which was certainly provocative or maybe I'd inhaled some of the opium which put me in a receptive mood but, no matter the cause, I sat listening to him, fascinated, not wanting him to stop."[49] So Gore had sat on Denny's bed, listening, absorbing.

With his eyes shut (the opium made them sensitive to light), Elliott asked Peter about himself. Peter told him about growing up in Toledo, Ohio, his work at Columbia for his doctorate, his plans to marry Helen and teach — in short, his plans for a typical, all-American life — "but as I talked I couldn't help but think how dull my life must sound to Elliott. I cut it short. I couldn't compete with him."[50] Here is a first subtle sign that Peter finds his new acquaintance of special interest.

A pivotal point in the short story, and perhaps in Vidal's life, is revealed in the entry from the abandoned journal for May 29, 1948. Peter and Elliott are having dinner together. (In an oral history, Vidal spoke of dining with Denny a number of times after their first meeting in Denny's bedroom.) The two characters in the story begin to reveal more about themselves to each other:

> Eating fresh sole from the Channel, I told Elliott all about Jimmie, told him things I myself had nearly forgotten, had wanted to forget. I told him how it had started at twelve and gone on, without plan or thought or even acknowledgment until, at seventeen, I went to the Army and he to the Marines and a quick death. After the Army, I met Helen and forgot him completely; his death ... took with it all memory, a thousand summer days abandoned on a coral island.[51]

Here, in a style reminiscent of Hemingway's reliance on what is left out of a story, what is not told, to give it emotional depth, is the Jimmie Trimble story. Gore already had told Tennessee Williams all about Jimmie, and Christopher Isherwood's diaries from these days reveal that Vidal had told him of his love for Jimmie.[52] That he would share this story with Denny when they were together hints at the intimacies of their conversation.

Finishing his story, Peter wonders why he had told Elliott, feeling as if he had said too much: why was he telling his new acquaintance that which revealed the innermost secrets he had not even acknowledged to himself? Elliott contemplated silently what he had heard, then spoke to Peter "about life and duty to oneself and how the moment is all one has and how it is dishonorable to cheat oneself of that." Peter thinks about this "strange disjointed speech." As he writes in his journal: "I'm not sure that he said anything very useful or very original but sitting there in the dark, listening, his words had a peculiar urgency for me and I felt, in a way, that I was listening to an oracle . . ."[53]

Could this be the turning point when Peter/Gore came to grips with their own identity, their own sexuality, who they were? Could Denny have had that sort of impact on Gore's life? Does Vidal's fragmentary locked-away journal from this year contain this sort of personal revelation so that he did not want the journal opened until long after his death?

Six years later Peter, who by then had acknowledged his sexuality, learns of Elliott's death, which brings back to him memories of those months in 1948: "what an important summer that was, the chrysalis burst at last. . ."[54]

In itself, "Pages from an Abandoned Journal" is not a memorable short story, certainly not one that would have found its way into an anthology of the best short stories of the decade, or even one that would be remembered long after it is read.

Nevertheless, it's an intriguing story that may be read on a number of levels. It is a subtly unfolding, finally wrought coming-of-age story of Peter's awakening to his sexuality, his identity, with Elliott perhaps as a catalyst who opened his eyes – the oracle – to the importance of being true to oneself, of the importance of the moment. This story adheres so closely to the details of Denny's life that it perhaps is not a reckless leap to conclude that it is a close transcription of the secret pages from Vidal's journal locked away with his papers at Harvard. In all of his voluminous and often introspective writings, Vidal never analyzes his transformation from the man at the Christmas party at Mrs. Shippen's Dancing School that December in 1942, telling Jimmie Trimble of his plans to marry Rosalind while "coming simultaneously" with Jimmie in the basement men's room stall, to the man who lived with Howard Austen from 1952 until his partner's death in 2003. Did Vidal's encounters with Denham Fouts hold the key to his own awakening, the time when his own "chrysalis burst"? Certainly the year 1948, the year he repeatedly called that "annus mirabilis," a time when "those of us who had missed our youth tried to catch up,"[55] had a special meaning in his life. If so, this obscure, quiet short story may someday be viewed as central to Gore Vidal's life story, and as a nonfiction chronicle of a memorable character, Denham Fouts.

A CHARACTER IN SEARCH OF AN AUTHOR: THE LAST LORD TREDGAR

EVAN MORGAN WAS THE ONLY SON of the third Lord Tredegar — Courtenay Morgan—and of the Lady Katherine Agnes Blanche Carnegie. The old Tredegar family fortune in coal funded a 121,000 acre estate in Monmouthshire (Gwent) in south Wales, as well as entire city streets in London. Their sprawling seventeenth century country house was one of the most magnificent in Great Britain, with its paneled rooms, windows framed by heavy velvet draperies, state rooms lit by hundreds of candles casting light and shadows on coats of arms, massive gold-framed family portraits, and elaborate molded ceilings inset with oval paintings. Tredegar House was run by a staff of forty-five who lived and worked in the mansion, with more in charge of the grounds, the brewery, the bakery, the gardens. There were housemaids, groomsmen, an indoor gardener, a hall boy, stickmen to provide wood for the many fireplaces, housekeepers, coachmen, valets, footmen, a lodge keeper, bricklayer, stone mason, scullery maid, deer keeper, kennel keeper--a small army of servants, some of whom were the third and fourth generations to live and work on the estate.

Evan's father passed his time in the usual pursuits of the landed gentry — hunting, shooting, fishing and sailing his steam yacht, *Liberty*, one of thelargest private yachts afloat. He was proficient at each pastime, but his real goal was in getting away from Tredegar House as frequently as possible, for the Lady Katherine had come to believe she was — a bird — a kingfisher to be exact — and had built for herself a large nest in one of the mansion's sitting rooms. And there she sat, wearing a cloth beak.

What chance would a boy have growing up in this home? Evan quite predictably was quite an eccentric. "Evan's misfortune," one friend said, "was to have been born with far too much money . . . and no practical sense at all."[1] Evan, who fancied himself a poet, mingled with the authors and artists of the day, some of whom painted vivid word portraits of their wealthy acquaintance. Poet and author Nancy Cunard called Evan "a fantasy who could be most charming and most bitchy."[2] Aldous Huxley reported to a friend that "I like him, I think, quite a lot, tho' he is the most fearfully spoilt child." [3] Going for a walk during a visit at Garsington in November of 1917, Virginia Woolf encountered a car "full of speckled and not prepossessing young men . . . The most obvious was Evan Morgan, a little red absurdity, with a beak of a nose, no chin, and a general likeness to a very callow but student Bantam cock, who has run to legs & neck. However, he was evidently most carefully prepared to be a poet & an eccentricity, both by his conversation, which aimed at irresponsible brilliance, & lack of reticence, & by his clothes, which must have been copied from the usual Shelley picture. But he was as innocent as a chicken & so foolish it didn't seem to matter."[4] An acquaintance described him as being "tall and very thin, with odd articulated movements, as if preparing to spread wings in flight."[5] His voice "had a lilt to it, and his speech was often broken by a snort as he took another pinch of snuff. He appeared utterly confident, utterly relaxed . . . but very evidently a man of vivid caprice . . ."[6] Evan at the time served as the unpaid secretary to the Parliamentary secretary of the Ministry of Labour.

It was in London at the Restaurant de la Tour Eiffel on Percy Street off Tottenham Court Road, a restaurant popular both with the aristocracy and the artistic set, that Evan met with this coterie of poets, painters, authors, actors and musicians — Duff Cooper, Nancy Cunard, Whydham Lewis, Michael Arlen, George Bernard Shaw, Igor Stravinsky, August John, Aldous Huxley, Dylan Thomas, the Sitwells. Cheerleader and instigator of this group dubbed by the press the "Bright Young People," Evan, never one to tolerate boredom, devised adventures for his group such as a midnight treasure hunt in London in which the participants had a list of objects to find and bring to a 2 a.m. party, or dinners to which the guests came dressed as young children and acted accordingly. [7] A young man at one of Evan's events remembered how it "began at the Eiffel Tower [restaurant] and ended at somebody's bedroom at Prince's Hotel in Jermyn Street" and how, at that point, he left abruptly "clutching my remaining bits of virtue — bundled them into a taxi and trundled home. I've never seen anything so stupendously naughty, even in Oxford! Never again — as I value my reputation."[8]

Evan's mother, worried about her son, offered to pay all expenses for Aldous Huxley, then teaching at Eton, to chaperone him on a trip abroad, hoping, as Huxley put it to a friend, "that my respectable middle-aged temperament would act as a slight brake to Evan's whirligig habits." The inability to get a wartime passport prevented their travels, but Huxley witnessed an example of these "whirligig habits" the very next day while at the studio of an artist "spasmodically trying to paint a nude study from a very lovely little model with red hair . . . Evan and the model became increasingly affectionate."[9]

One of the Bright Young People, the popular novelist Ronald Firbank, had set his sights on Evan, who had filled out a little since Virginia Woolf had viewed him as a "student Bantam cock," doe-eyed Evan with his wavy light brown hair and sensuous lips. Evan at first was fascinated by his conversations with the older Firbank, conversations, as he characterized them, "of a most speculative and dubious character,"[10] conversations which made Evan feel that his admirer was "under the influence of Bacchus . . . at least you could never tell because his conversation was equally wild either way."[11] One friend noted Ronald "spoke only in strangled and disjointed gasps of rapture, hilarity and dismay."[12] He wore, Evan observed, shirts of a color "never seen off the stage" and his ties were "very bohemian."[13] But it was his hands that most troubled Evan, those well groomed nails with a deep carmine polish, those hands, one could never tell where they might "find themselves."[14]

Evan was amused by Ronald and viewed him "as one might some rare bird to be cherished for its exquisite exotic qualities rather than as a human being"[15], but his amusement began to turn to concern when he realized that Ronald was cherishing him in a very different way, (Ronald's nickname for Evan was "Heaven Organ")[16], and those troublesome hands kept finding themselves in the wrong places.

Twenty-seven year old Evan dutifully told his father that his relationship with Ronald was becoming of "deep concern" to him, and noted how Ronald had a habit of "running his fingers through his hair, just like a woman my dear" leading to some "sinister suspicions concerning him."[17] Ronald proudly had told Evan of his plan to dedicate to him his latest novel, *The Princess Zouburoff*, with a dedication that would read: "To the Hon. Evan Morgan in Souvenir Amicale of a 'Previous Incarnation.'"[18] (When Ronald first met Evan, he told him that his profile was identical to that of the mummy of Ramses, and that he must be a reincarnation of the ancient Egyptian pharaoh). This was a little much, especially since Evan was finding himself attracted not to Ronald but to another member of his coterie, the composer Philip Heseltine, a friend from his Eton and Oxford days. Aghast at Firbank's proposed dedication, Evan had his father instruct the family solicitors to intercede and communicate to Firbank that should his new book ever be published with that dedication, Evan Morgan would "take such steps as he may be advised to protect his interest and to make his views on the subject perfectly clear to the public and his friends."[19] The publisher had the dedication page physically cut from each book before it was released.

Other fathers were warning their sons about Evan, just as Lord Tredegar cautioned Evan about Ronald. While a student at Eton, Alan Pryce- Jones' father had taken him aside in his library and said "You are old enough to know that there exists a man named Evan Morgan. He is a first cousin of your friend Pinhead. And I tell you here and now that should you ever find yourself in the same room, you are to leave immediately."[20] "Why?," Alan innocently asked his father, who responded that "he would tell me one day . . . one day when I was older." Ominous words, to be sure, and words that Alan's father never elaborated upon; and of course Alan's response was to pester Pinhead immediately to introduce him to Evan Morgan. Pinhead did and "we took to one another at once" and they became friends. "I had no reason to be other than grateful to him for as much affection as his leprechaun character would bestow on a friend."[21] Another young man worried about a *Vogue* portrait that showed him standing next to Evan Morgan: "The ravishing beauty of my face and my figure rendered my proximity to this old starfish most suspicious to the ignorant."[22]

It had not been so many years before that Oscar Wilde had been sentenced to two years of hard labor in Reading Gaol for the attraction he felt toward Bosie, Lord Alfred Douglas. Evan, a good friend of Lord Alfred, whom he considered "the greatest sonneteer since Shakespeare,"[23] was very much aware of this when he contemplated Ronald Firbank's feelings toward him, and his own toward Philip Heseltine.

It was just at this point in his life that Evan took up the notion of becoming a priest, and became the first Tredegar in five centuries to join the Roman Catholic Church. After he had one of the family's Rolls Royces fitted with an altar, his chauffeur drove him to Rome where he entered the Vatican seminary. Perhaps it was because he sent his valet to attend all his classes and take notes that he never did become a priest, but certainly all was not lost. In 1923, at the age of thirty, he was made the Privy Chamberlain of the Sword and Cape by Pope Benedict XV, (and continued in the same office under Pope Pius XI), an office which entailed spending a few weeks in the Vatican each year performing ceremonial duties, and which entitled him to flamboyant robes which he wore for his formal portrait which hung at Tredegar House, and which, in fact, he wore whenever possible. His friend Nancy Cunard remembered seeing Evan in Rome dressed as "some sort of papal chamberlain" wearing something that to her resembled "a British admiral's uniform--the hat particularly."[24] Another friend described him as "an 18th century figure come to life again."[25] And later Gore Vidal recalled seeing him carrying "a big attaché case with the Tredegar coat of arms, more elaborate than the Queen of England's."[26] Evan's religious convictions were erratic at best. He once owned a relic of the true Cross, but mislaid it in an all male Turkish bath.

Evan's sister, Gwyneth, had drowned in the Thames — a drug related suicide, it was rumored. Evan was ordered by his father to marry and produce an heir. Ideas of the priesthood abandoned, thirty-five year old Evan, in 1928, married Lois Sturt (a "most unwilling bride" one friend observed),[27] the strikingly beautiful daughter of the 2nd Baron Alington and Lady Feodorowna Yorke. As Gore Vidal noted, this "glamorous Mountbatten world" was "boldly bisexual. Bloomsbury with coronets. And everybody got married."[28] Lois had been a film star in the early 1920s and had been the lover of the 15th Earl of Pembroke and of Prince George, the duke of Kent, soon to become King George VI of England. Prince George had wanted to marry her, but the royal family opposed the union due to her "fast" reputation.

It was on the world travels of this couple — who were often, as a friend commented in "remote communication" — that Evan happened to spot Denham Fouts being escorted by the police through the lobby of the Quisisana Hotel on Capri for not paying his hotel bills.

"Unhand that handsome youth," Evan commanded the police, "he is mine." [29]

And so it was that Denny Fouts, who Truman Capote later would call "the best kept boy in the world," become part of Evan's entourage.

Was Evan's wife concerned when her husband so suddenly made a new friend who was now joining them as they continued the Grand Tour, or did she consider this just another manifestation of Evan's charming eccentricities, another addition to his unusual collection of acquaintances? In China, they visited the opium dens where Denny sampled the wares and developed a life-long addiction.

When Evan's father died, Evan became Lord Tredegar, a viscount and baron, lord of five hundred year old Tredegar House. And then the real fun began.

The glitterati, along with the beautiful and the handsome unknowns, made their way to his infamous weekend garden parties at Tredegar Park: H.G. Wells, Marchesa Casati, Aleister Crowley, Lord Alfred Douglas, Lady Nancy Cunard, the painter August John, George Bernard Shaw, William Butler Yeats, G.K. Chesterton, Aldous Huxley. Denny Fouts was right at home in this glamorous party world at one of the grandest manors of the English-speaking world.

In addition to the menagerie of guests, Evan had assembled at his estate a menagerie of animals. There was Somerset, the boxing kangaroo with which Evan invariably boxed a few rounds at each party, Alice the honey bear, Blue Boy, a rather frightening macaw which perched on Evan's shoulder spitting out obscenities and which seemed to have a particular dislike for H.G. Wells, attacking the famed author with hammer-like blows, baboons that stalked and terrified the hapless gardeners, anteaters, pigeons, birds of prey, falcons and owls which Evan trained to swoop over the guests. He would call "Rosa, Rosa" and Rosa, a duck, would fly straight to him from the other side of the lake in the park; as a friend noted, "birds came crowding round him like spinsters round a popular preacher."[30] To the delight of his guests, he had trained Blue Boy to climb up his leg inside his trousers and push its beak out through his buttoned fly.[31]

Drink and drugs fueled these circus-like gatherings. "He's one of the very few people I know who can throw a party," one of the guests, Aleister Crowley, recorded in admiration in his diary.[32] Another guest, the socialite Sir Henry "Chips" Channon, MP, wrote in his diary that Tredegar House had "the feel and even smell of decay, of aristocracy in extremis, the sinister and the trivial, crucifixes and crocodiles . . ."[33]

Among the guests at Evan's weekend parties was Crown Prince Paul of Greece, living in exile in England since 1924 when the Greek Assembly had abolished the monarchy and declared Greece a republic. From that time, members of the royal family were forbidden to live in Greece, and twenty- three year old Paul and his older brother, King George II, had sought refuge in London. Paul, an athletic man, tall, broad-shouldered, with a jovial laugh and ready smile, on a lark had assumed an alias and found a job in a London factory constructing airplanes, though most of his time was spent moving in the upper social circles. And one weekend, at a party at Tredegar House, the prince met Denny Fouts.

As captivated by Denny as was Lord Tredegar, Prince Paul took Denny with him on a cruise around the Mediterranean. "We had some great times together on a yacht," Denny always would remember as he took out photograph albums to show his friends. And there Denny was, looking "very glamorous in belted white swimming trunks, leaning with merited narcissism against a lifebelt, upon some swaying Aegean deck."[34]

Lord Tredegar's wife died in 1937. Evan did have a knack of marrying well. In Singapore on March 13, 1939, forty-six year old Evan married twenty-four year old Princess Olga Sergeievna Dolgorousky from a family of Russian nobility that, before the Revolution, had been close to the Imperial family. Their marriage was annulled after three years on the grounds of his non-consummation. It appeared to have been a rather unhappy marriage that included an incident in which Evan tried to set fire to his wife.[35]

Through his family's standing, Evan found himself at the outset of the Second World War just where he didn't belong: in MI_5, Britain's esteemed counter-intelligence agency. Thinking well outside the box, his first scheme was to have peregrine falcons, like the ones he had trained at Tredegar Park to entertain the guests at his garden parties, attack German carrier pigeons and thereby disrupt the flow of classified information to pre-invasion agents. It was never clear just how the falcons would distinguish enemy pigeons from neutral pigeons, or develop a taste for Nazi pigeons more than other avian delicacies flying the skies at the same time.

This scheme morphed into a plan to slow the German push into France and Belgium by letting loose a massive flock of pigeons which would mingle with the Nazi carrier pigeons and confuse the Germans as to which pigeons were theirs. The RAF gave it a try with a squadron of planes taking off with cargo holds full of thousands of pigeons. Over the southern coast of England, the pigeons dropped from the planes were instantly de-feathered by the intake of the engines. Evan refined his plan. The next time the pigeons were taken aloft, they were in individual brown paper bags, the bags were let loose over the coast, and by the time the pigeons burst from the bags they at least were free of the planes; but rather than traveling to mingle with their fascist counterparts, they hurried back home to their familiar roosts.

Despite these setbacks, Evan was quite proud of his work as commander of the Falcon Interceptor Unit of MI_5, and one day, as he lunched with Lady Baden-Powell, broke all edicts of the counterintelligence agency by showing her around his office and describing in detail the war efforts in which he was involved. This was a blatant violation of the oath of secrecy he had taken, and Evan at once was arrested and imprisoned in the Tower of London. In due course, he was freed, and, fuming, made his way back to Tredegar Park.

Evan was not about to let the matter pass. He knew just who to contact to plan suitable revenge against those who summarily had imprisoned him: the infamous sixty-eight year old Aleister Crowley, a character the British tabloids had dubbed the "Beast of the Apocalypse," the "King of Depravity": the "Wickedest Man on Earth."

Crowley, who fancied himself, with Shakespeare, one of the two greatest poets of the English language, held himself out as a prophet of a new era that would supplant Christianity, an era when men would become gods. The central credo of his ministry was — "Do what thou wilt shall be the whole of the law" — a credo which focused on individual freedom while flirting with license and anarchy. A mystic, a spiritual philosopher who fiddled with the concept of reality, Crowley considered magick (as he spelled it to distinguish it from pedestrian tricks of magic) "the science and art of causing change in conformity with will."[36] His rituals and sacraments, in which genital secretions served the same role as the wine and wafer, included the use of hashish, mescaline, heroin and opium, sexual magick with both male and female partners, and the consumption of the blood of cats.

Crowley was a student of occultism, and his devotion to magic and mysticism paralleled Evan's, who before the War had been a member of the "Black Hand," a private occult society in London, and who recently had been constructing, at great cost, an elaborate magic temple on his estate. Surely here was just the person to help perform a little black magick to bring about the revenge against his arresting officer that Evan craved.

The two conspirators were kindred spirits. Crowley had been a guest at many of Evan's notorious weekend parties and had inscribed one of his books, *The Book of Thoth*, to Evan as follows:

"To my old and very dear Friend and Colleague, Adept of Adepts in the Secret Tradition, Eifon Morgan, heir of the Mysteries of the Round Table, entitled to bear Excalibur, Lord of the Secret Marches about Camelot do I, being the pupil and heir of Merlin, entrust this Book, Aleister Crowley."[37] So Evan was well aware of just what havoc Crowley could wreak when on May 18, 1943, he wrote to the Great Beast, inviting him to come stay at Tredegar Park. Crowley arrived on June 17, and was housed in the Oak Room, the grandest in the mansion, a forty-two foot long bedroom that once had been the main state dining room of Tredegar House, with its massive fireplace and seventeenth century oak paneling carved with busts of the Roman emperors, scrolls of acanthus leaves and grotesque heads. On Sunday, June 20, 1943, Crowley wrote in his diary: "Saw T's Magick room--far greater than I thought."[38] That was saying something.

Crowley stayed at Tredegar Park for two weeks to carry out his work. Exactly what sort of black magic the two concocted, what spells cast, what séances conducted, is not known, though the conspirators were suitably smug when, soon after the Great Beast's visit, they learned that the officer who had had Evan thrown into the Tower of London was beset with a painful illness that brought him satisfyingly close to death.

The War years were not kind to Evan. Quite predictably, managing his estate and fortune was not his strong suit. By the end of the War, it suddenly hit him that with his excessive spending, coupled with excessively rising wartime taxes, he was financially ruined. In 1945, he had the family silver at Tredegar House transported to an auction house in London to be sold.

His family's reputation continued to bail him out of a series of compromising situations as the police organized sting operations to crack down on homosexual activities. At the same time, he was contemplating a third marriage; there was no end to women who believed that they could seduce and convert him and end up with the title: Lady Tredegar. But it all came to an end when he was diagnosed with terminal cancer and on April 27, 1949 died at the age of 56.

As his friend. Aldous Huxley, summed up so strange a life: "Why even bother trying to make up characters for books when real people like Evan Morgan already exist."[39]

DE GUSTIBUS NON EST DISPUTANDUM:

On the Folly of Reviewing Books

ONCE AN AUTHOR'S MANUSCRIPT has made its arduous, improbable journey upstream and is accepted for publication, it must once again strike out alone against the current, out of the control of its author, agent, editor and publisher, seeking a nod now from the reviewers, and a favorable nod at that. To a frightening degree on that favorable nod now rides the fate of the book — frightening because whether the nod is favorable depends so much on the vagaries of chance.

John Updike and Paul Theroux — prolific writers, sophisticated authors, certainly distinguished men of letters — both reviewed Erica Jong's *Fear of Flying* when it was published in 1973.

Updike's review began: "Erica Jong's first novel feels like a winner. It has class and sass, brightness and bite. Containing all the cracked eggs of the feminist litany, her soufflé rises with a poet's afflatus. She sprinkles on the four-letter words as if women had invented them; her cheerful sexual frankness brings a new flavor to female prose … Fearless and fresh, tender and exact, Mrs. Jong has arrived nonstop at the point of being a literary personality … "[1]

Paul Theroux's comments were quite different: "With such continual and insistent reference to her cherished valve, Erica Jong's witless heroine looms like a mammoth pudendum, as roomy as the Carlsbad Caverns, luring amorous spelunkers to confusion in her plunging grottoes. On her eighth psychoanalyst and second marriage, Isadora Wing admits to a contortion we are not privileged to observe and confesses, 'I seem to live inside my cunt,' which strikes one as a choice as inconvenient as a leaky bedsitter in Elmer's End." And on he goes, calling the book a "crappy novel."[2]

"A winner"? "A crappy novel"? Say what?

Happens all the time.

A review in the *New York Times* of April 24, 2016 savaged a new biography of the poet Wallace Stevens, "*The Whole Harmonium,*" dubbing it "doubly disappointing" — "an undramatic, literal-minded chronicle; essentially a long, strenuous paraphrase of Stevens' writing, with thin strips of quotation laid on the gridiron of chronology."

A week later, on May 2, a four page review in *The New Yorker* praised it to the skies as "a thrilling story of a mind," a "superb biography" by an author "who has a prehensile feel for the roots and branches of literary modernism, exemplary taste in what he chooses to quote, and a real gift for exegesis, unpacking poems in language that is nearly as eloquent as the poet's, and as clear as faithfulness allows" in chapters that "sparkle with personalities, anecdotes and ideas."

Look at Kenneth Roberts' diary entry for December 9, 1937: "Learned that *Northwest Passage* had been the choice of the English Book Society, and that they had spoken with enthusiasm of the English scenes in it. This was pleasing, since Allan Nevins, in his review of *Northwest Passage*, had pontifically said that my handling of the English scenes had been painfully inadequate, and that I wasn't competent to write about Englishmen of culture or refinement."[3]

Nabokov's *Lolita* was hailed by Elizabeth Janeway in her review in the *New York Times Book Review*: "The first time I read *Lolita* I thought it was one of the funniest books I'd ever come on … The second time I read it, uncut, I thought it was one of the saddest … Humbert is every man who is driven by desire, wanting his Lolita so badly that it never occurs to him to consider her as a human being, or as anything but a dream-figment made flesh

… As for pornographic content, I can think of few volumes more likely to quench the flames of lust than this exact and immediate description of its consequences." Orville Prescott had his say the next day in a review in the daily *New York Times*: "Lolita, then, is undeniably news in the world of books. Unfortunately, it is bad news. There are two equally serious reasons it isn't worth any adult reader's attention. The first is that it is dull, dull in a pretentious, florid and archly fatuous fashion. The second is that it is repulsive … highbrow pornography."[4]

In the *New York Times* of January 25, 1990, Christopher Lehmann-Haupt aired his disappointment in P.D. James's eleventh novel, *Devices and Desires*. He felt that the plot's "chain reaction of false leads, dead ends, subverted logic and clumsy comings and goings" reduced the novel "to a conventional who dunnit" with "lengthy descriptive passages that fail to justify the space they take up" and with "silly over-explanatory dialogue that reads like bloated word-balloons floating out of a void." How much worse could it get? Let's see. "Not even as a maze with no way out does the story make much sense … We come to understand that the show must go on. But we find only a slight reason to attend it." So there!

But then, three days later, on the front page of the *New York Times Book Review*, appeared another review of the book. Now, to garner both a weekday and a Sunday *Times* review is the sign of an important book. And it is instructive to compare the two. The Sunday review was by the distinguished film critic Judith Crist, who had been a judge for the annual Edgar Awards of the Mystery Writers of America. Her opinion of the book was as clear in her opening sentence as Lehmann- Haupt's had been in his last: "Her newest mystery, *Devices and Desires*, is P.D. James at better than her best."

Whoa! Wait just a minute!

Were Mr. Lehmann-Haupt and Ms. Crist sent the same bound

galleys by P.D. James's publisher? Surely another publishing mix-up, right? Wrong. Ms. Crist goes on: "She offers her readers the satisfactions of an artfully constructed, beautifully written story of flesh-and-blood individuals in a time and place we get to know as well as the inhabitants. Not, mind you, that she ignores the conventions of the mystery story: the crime, the clues, the suspects and the puzzlement are there, but so absorbing a read does she offer that final revelations seem almost a bonus."

Assuming these two well-respected critics were reading the same book, who was right and who was wrong? Whose judgment was better? Both reviews were well written and well reasoned. No matter to P.D. James, for both prominent reviews undoubtedly helped the sales of her book.

How can these sorts of conflicting reviews be reconciled? Peter Benchley, whose *Jaws* did not receive the sort of reviews for which he had hoped, noted, after the dust had settled, "I still don't understand how a book can get raves from one reviewer and be considered garbage by another."[5]

De Gustibus non est disputandum. "In matters of taste, there can be no disputes."

Right. But tell that to the author of a first novel who doesn't get two reviews in the *New York Times*, who gets one short review if he's lucky, very lucky, and that one review happens to be like the Christopher Lehmann-Haupt review of *Devices and Desires*, with no Judith Crist riding in on a white steed to save the day with another view. Then what? Barring a miracle, that is the end of that book. And that might well be the end of that writing career.

It does not take a whole lot of evidence to demonstrate just how outlandishly wrong eminent critics have been.

Reviewers had not a clue, for example, what to make of *The Great Gatsby*, though the *Saturday Review of Literature* was sure that "Mr. F. Scott Fitzgerald deserves a good shaking ... *The Great Gatsby* is an absurd story, whether considered as romance, melodrama, or plain record of New York high life." The *New York Herald Tribune* agreed: "What has never been alive cannot very well go on living. So this is a book of the season only . . ."[6] Tell that to Scribners: to this day, almost a century after publication, Fitzgerald's masterpiece remains its bestselling title each year.

Writing in *The New Yorker*, Clifton Fadiman called William Faulkner's *Absalom, Absalom!* "The final blowup of what was once a remarkable, if minor, talent."[7]

The *New York Times Book Review* concluded that Joseph Heller's *Catch-22* "gasps for want of craft and sensibility ... The book is an emotional hodgepodge; no mood is sustained long enough to register for more than a chapter."[8]

And Stanley Kauffmann, writing in *The New Republic*, dismissed Truman Capote's *In Cold Blood*: "One can say of this book – with sufficient truth to make it worth saying: 'This isn't writing. It's research.'"[9]

If eminent critics can miss the boat, can one review really make or break a book?

Alfred A. Knopf recalled that when he was a young man, "Mencken, William Lyon Phelps, Heywood Broun, Burton Rascoe, and Henry Sell — the latter two writing in Chicago — to name only five, *could* secure an almost immediate hearing for a book in which they believed — sometimes, as in Mencken's case, by denouncing it so brilliantly and provocatively that people rushed to read it."[10] Anais Nin was publishing her books with a home printing press, and then through tiny presses, when Edmund Wilson got hold of one and wrote a glowing review for *The New Yorker*. "It launched me," Nin declared. "Immediately all the publishers were ready to reprint both books in commercial editions."[11] And Malcom Cowley didn't attribute the revival of an interest in Faulkner's work to his *Faulkner Por-*

table, but rather to a front page review of the book in the *New York Times* and a major review in *The New Republic*.[12] So yes, a review can make a book.

A bad review, even in a prominent publication, will not always break a book. The panning in the *New York Times Book Review* of *Scarlett*, the sequel to Margaret Mitchell's *Gone With the Wind* ("My best advice to GWTW fans is 'Don't bother ... This is dreadful ... You'll be really mad at yourself if you waste money buying it"[13]) put not a dent in the enormous sales of the book. According to the *Wall Street Journal*, "no other novel in the history of the printed word sold so many copies as quickly"[14] — 1.2 million hardcovers sold in six weeks. Nor could all the reviewers' sticks and stones break any bones of a James Michener (a review of Michener's *Journey* in the *New York Times Book Review* noted that it "is not absolute junk. But I suspect no one but James Michener could get it published"[15]), or a Judith Krantz or a Danielle Steel or a Stephen King (a snide review in *Time* of his novel *The Dark Half* — "in each genre there is good trash and bad trash, and King's does not seem very good"[16] — probably didn't affect one bit the sales of the first printing of 1.5 million). Their books have lives of their own. Reviewers can pound them as much as they wish and not harm their sales.

On the other hand, one review in the *New York Times* indeed may break a book. Is it indeed true, as an editor-in-chief of a major publishing house once remarked, that: "I greatly welcome a review in the *Times* no matter whether it is favorable or not; any review [in the *New York Times*] sells books." [17]?

Really?

Tell that to John Cheever, whose third novel, *Bullet Park*, was picked apart on the front page of the *New York Times Book Review* of April 27, 1969, by Benjamin DeMott, a professor of English at Amherst. "The manuscript was received enthusiastically everywhere,"

Cheever reported, "but when Benjamin DeMott dumped on it in the *Times*, everybody picked up their marbles and went home."[18] The book sold only 33,000 hardcover copies. Tell that to Gore Vidal, who early in his career saw the power of the *New York Times* to make or break a writer. His first novel, *Williwaw* (1946), was praised by the powerful *New York Times* critic Orville Prescott. "I was made," Vidal remembers.[19] Two years later his next novel appeared, *The City and the Pillar*, which dealt with a homosexual relationship. Prescott read the book and was horrified, telling Vidal's publisher, "I will not only never review another novel by this disgusting writer, but I will never read one."[20] Vidal's next five novels were not reviewed in the *Times*. "I was unmade. For ten years I did television, theater, movies" before returning to the novel.[21]

Vidal saw the same power of the *Times* years later, in 1976, when he reviewed Tennessee Williams' *Memoirs*. "We had been friends from the late forties to the early sixties . . . When next we met, he narrowed his cloudy blue eyes and said, in tones that one of these biographers would call 'clipped,' 'When your review appeared my book was number five on the nonfiction best-seller list of the *New York Times*. Within two weeks of your review, it was not listed at all.'"[22]

"Time is the only critic without ambition," John Steinbeck once said.[23] And maybe time, and not the *Times*, is the real critic, the real judge of a book's worth. After all, Malcolm Cowley's *Exile's Return* was shattered by hostile reviews when it was published in 1934, selling a grand total of 983 copies; it was reissued in 1951 and took off, becoming a classic. James Agee's *Let Us Now Praise Famous Men* shared a similar history, selling a handful of copies when published to bad reviews in 1941, but recognized as a masterpiece by the 1960s.

In today's publishing world, however, a book may disappear — yes disappear from the face of the earth — before time has had its chance to render its verdict. "I cannot greatly care what the critics say of my work," John Updike once remarked; "if it is good, it will come to the surface in a generation or two or float, and if not, it will sink, having in the meantime provided me with a living, the opportunities of leisure, and a craftsman's intimate satisfactions."[24] Now maybe that was true for John Updike (though Mary McCarthy revealed that she almost didn't read Updike's *Rabbit, Run* because of the reviews, but when she did get around to it she found it "the most interesting American novel I've read in quite a long time"[25]); but if all of Updike's readers were put off by a negative review, he perhaps would have found his books providing him more intimate satisfactions and less of a living. As May Sarton succinctly put it, "A bad review keeps readers from buying a book, it is as simple as that."[26]

Not so long ago, a new book might remain in a bookstore for a year, eighteen months, two years, before being sent back to the publisher. Not so today when, as Calvin Trillin reminds us, the average shelf life of a trade book is "somewhere between milk and yogurt."[27] Promotion and word of mouth have to work pretty darn fast to get a book selling, and a well-placed, ill-natured, silly review can bludgeon a good book to death.

How? Very simply. Most commercial publishers don't implement their advertising plans for the majority of their books — those not by a "name" author, not by a celebrity, and not focused on the events on today's front page – until the reviews start coming in. If an early review in a key publication (the *New York Times* is the prime example) is unfavorable, the publishers are spooked, stop publicity and promotion and move on to another book. As a result, the bookstores stop ordering, the radio and television talk shows stop calling, the newspaper and magazines look elsewhere for stories, reviewers stop reviewing, paperback houses and television and movie studios don't bid, and the public, never having had the chance to hear about the book, doesn't buy. Just like that, the book an author has slaved over for years is no more. According to John Cheever, Knopf had anticipated that his *Bullet Park* would be a best-seller. "There was a hostile review in the *Times* and the publisher stopped all advertising."[28] And so, the book was not a best-seller or even a fair seller.

This is the catch-22 of publishing. Many publishers have concluded that advertising, to be effective, must follow sales, that sales don't follow advertising; so a book must prove itself without advertising before it can get a piece of a publisher's advertising budget. Yet how, without advertising, can anyone know the book exists? The answer, of course, is reviews.

So authors bite their nails, and wait: "I should be working, but now I wait for reviews," John Cheever wrote, anticipating the first notices of one of his novels. "I not only wait for them: I write them. I've written them all, even the Albany Times- Union."[29]

And they feel rotten when the reviews aren't good: "I never felt worse in my life," Kurt Vonnegut recalled when every review – from the *New York Times*, to *Time*, *Newsweek*, *The New York Review of Books*, the *Village Voice*, and *Rolling Stone* — panned his *Slapstick*. "I felt as though I were sleeping standing up in a boxcar in Germany again."[30]

And they fall into despair. Upon reading some hostile reviews, Thomas Wolfe wrote from Geneva, Switzerland, to his editor, Max Perkins: "Will you please have Mr. Darrow [Whitney Darrow, vice president of Scribners] send me a statement of whatever money is due me? I shall not write any more books, and since I must begin to make other plans for the future, I should like to know how much money I will have."[31]

Ernest Hemingway had the same reaction. "I am tempted never to publish another damned thing. The swine aren't worth writing for. I swear to Christ they're not. Every phase of the whole racket is so disgusting that it makes you feel like vomiting."[32] Malcolm Cowley, too. "It all seems amusing in retrospect, but the impression it gave me of being exposed and helpless, a criminal chained and taunted in the marketplace, was a shattering experience while it lasted ... I reviewed for the *New Republic* — with rather more kindness to authors than I had shown in the beginning, I wrote essays and poems, but for years I couldn't bring myself to write another book."[33]

And so, sometimes, just in this way, a bad review may bludgeon not only a book, but also a writing career.

What recourse does an author have when hit with an unfair review? Well, if you're Norman Mailer and receive such a review, as he did in 1991 from John Simon in the *New York Times Book Review* for his novel *Harlot's Ghost*, you can request (and get) a meeting with the editors of the *Times* to demonstrate how the reviewer was biased against you, and demand (and get) "prominent play" for a lengthy rebuttal. Nevertheless, that prominent play — in which Mailer marshalled more than sufficient evidence to demonstrate that Mr. Simon hated his guts — could not reverse the precipitous slip from its fingerhold on the *Times* Best Sellers list of the magnum opus on which he had labored for seven years, nor could it prevent the final word by "The Editor" at the end of his prominent play: that Mr. Simon "wrote a fair and balanced review that met the standards of this newspaper."[34]

Now suppose a criminal defendant were gagged during his trial and not represented by counsel. Suppose that jury promptly found this defendant guilty and the judge sentenced him to seven years imprisonment — all without a word in his own defense. You can bet that the *New York Times* would be all over that one, front page coverage, editorials, op eds, the works. Yet the *Times* has no problem letting a reviewer serve as prosecutor, judge, jury, and executioner of a book on which an author has toiled for years, with the author effectively gagged and unable to say so much as "Now just a minute."

Unless he's Norman Mailer — and even for Mailer things didn't work out so well — there's precious little an author can do (author Dan Moldea sued the *New York Times* — ultimately to no avail —

when the *Book Review* in 1989 trashed his book *Interference: How Organized Crime Influences Professional Football*), or maybe even should do, for there is nothing to be gained by answering a critic. It's a waste of psychic energy, a waste of time, and, as Saul Bellow recognized when he quoted the Jewish proverb that any fool can throw a stone into the water which ten wise men can't recover,[35] oftentimes an impossibility.

The brutalized author, though, need not just sit there and take it. Jean Kerr, author of *Please Don't Eat the Daisies*, had the best idea of how to deal with such assaults: "Confronted by an absolutely infuriating review it is sometimes helpful for the victim to do a little personal research on the critic. Is there any truth to the rumor that he had no formal education beyond the age of eleven? In any event, is he able to construct a simple English sentence? Do his participles dangle? When moved to lyricism does he write 'I had a fun time?' Was he ever arrested for burglary? I don't know that you will prove anything this way, but is perfectly harmless and quite soothing."[36]

At one time or another, most authors have followed this formula for relief. "Critics are like horse-flies which prevent the horse from ploughing," said Chekhov; "For over twenty years I have read criticism of my stories and I do not remember a single remark of any value or one word of valuable advice." These truths have persisted from Chekhov to Grisham: "I've sold too many books to get good reviews anymore," John Grisham has said. "There's a lot of jealousy, because [reviewers] think they can write a good novel or a best-seller and get frustrated when they can't. As a group, I've learned to despise them."[37] Wrote Samuel Taylor Coleridge: "Reviewers are usually people who would have been poets, historians, biographers, etc., if they could. They have tried their talents at one or at the other, and have failed; therefore they turn critics."[38] This sentiment was set to verse by James Russell Lowell:

Nature fits all her children with something to do;
He who would write and can't write, can surely review.[39]

Criticism is a tricky business, because what we bring to the reading of a book will shape our reactions to it. *When* a reader reads a book can be of significance, not only the particular day or time of day — a book might seem meaningless drivel if read in an oral surgeon's reception room, as it might seem truly enchanting if read on a lazy summer afternoon in a hammock under the shady branches of a tree — but also the particular time of life. A reader first encountering *The Catcher in the Rye* as a junior in high school might have no idea what Holden Caulfield's problem is. By the next year, he could be Holden. When rereading the book in his thirties, he might be dazzled by Salinger's art, by his extraordinary creation of life, something he had not appreciated in his first two readings. A fifty-eight-year-old reader picking up the book for the first time might discover little to recommend it, undoubtedly just why the reviewer for the *New York Herald Tribune Book Review* concluded about Salinger's novel: "Recent war novels have accustomed us all to ugly words and images, but from the mouths of the very young and protected they sound peculiarly offensive … The ear refuses to believe."[40]

"For a book to be great in a reader's life," John Updike said, "it is not enough for the book to be great; the reader must be ready."[41] Certain kinds of novels, he noted, "especially nineteenth-century novels, should be read in adolescence, on those dreamily endless solitary afternoons that in later life become so uselessly short and full of appointments, or they will never be read at all."[42] Similarly, Truman Capote believed that "between thirteen and sixteen are the ideal if not the only ages for succumbing to Thomas Wolfe — he seemed to me a great genius then, and still does, though I can't read a line of it now. Just as other youthful flames have guttered: Poe, Dickens, Stevenson. I love them in memory, but find them unreadable."[43] Capote remembered that "I also didn't like *Moby*

Dick the first time I read it, but then I was about thirteen. The second time I read it I was about thirty and somewhere along the line I liked it a great deal."[44] Critic Joseph Epstein has said it best: "In place of capsule comments telling readers what a book is about, I should tell them where a particular book might best be read: in airports, in bed, in bathtubs, at solitary meals, in the country, on the subway, etc. My list would specify at roughly what age a book ought to be read; no F. Scott Fitzgerald beyond thirty; no Chekhov before thirty; no Proust before forty; no James Joyce after fifty."[45]

Even an author's evaluation of his own work can shift. Chaucer and Kafka questioned the very worth of their writing. Others really didn't understand the place of their work; Melville was convinced that *Pierre; or, The Ambiguities* would be a popular best-seller to match his previous *Typee* and *Omoo*. He died believing himself a failure: "No man," he despaired, "ever hitched his wagon higher to a star or fell so low."[46] Dickens thought of *Great Expectations* as something of a comedy. Fitzgerald believed *Tender Is the Night* to be a more experimental work of prose than James Joyce's *Ulysses*. Joyce believed *Finnegans Wake* a simple novel. Leonard Woolf had to snatch Virginia Woolf's manuscripts away from her before she tore them to pieces. John Steinbeck found his work at times "to have the high purpose I set for it, and at other times it seems pedestrian and trite."[47] As he worked on the last chapter of his masterpiece, *The Grapes of Wrath*, he was discouraged: "I am sure of one thing – it isn't the great book I had hoped it would be. It's just a run- of-the-mill book. And the awful thing is that it is absolutely the best I can do."[48] James Dickey observed that "your opinion of your own work fluctuates wildly. Under the right circumstances you can pick up something that you've written and approve of it; you'll think it's good and that nobody could have done exactly the same thing. Under different circumstances, you'll look at exactly the same poem and say, 'My Lord, isn't that *boring*.'"[49]

Let's face it: There are books — good books, great books — that each of us will never appreciate. For whatever reason, they are simply not our cup of tea. "Three times in my life I have read through Shakespeare and Goethe from end to end," sighed Leo Tolstoy, "and I never could make out in which their charm consisted."[50] Others have felt the same w about Tolstoy's writing. Anthony Trollope wrote that *War and Peace* had "absolutely no plot — no contrived arrangement of incidents by which interest is excited."[51] And Rebecca West admitted she was "a heretic" about Tolstoy. "I really don't see *War and Peace* as a great novel because it seems constantly to be trying to prove that nobody who was in the war knew what was going on. Well, I don't know whoever thought they would ... that if you put somebody down in the wildest sort of mess they understand what's happening."[52] Unlike Truman Capote, Gore Vidal never came to appreciate Melville. "I do detest *Moby Dick*," Vidal declared, "and I never finished *Pierre; or, the Ambiguities*. But then, I don't like Melville's writing. It is windy and pretentious, it is bogus Shakespeare."[53] Katherine Anne Porter could not stomach the writings of F. Scott Fitzgerald: "I couldn't read him then and I can't read him now ... Not only didn't I like his writing, but I didn't like the people he wrote about. I thought they weren't worth thinking about, and I still think so."[54] Henry James found *Crime and Punishment* so dull he could not finish it, while Robert Louis Stevenson called it the greatest book he had read in ten years. Stephen King cannot read James Michener. And so it goes.

Now, consider this: What if *Moby Dick* were Herman Melville's just- published first novel, and the *New York Times* selected Gore Vidal to review it? What if it selected Truman Capote but before he was old enough to appreciate the book? What if the *Times* selects Katherine Anne Porter to review a first novel by an author named F. Scott Fitzgerald? What if the reviewer assigned a first novel is running out of time to meet the deadline to have his review in to the *Times*, and takes the manuscript with him to his appointment with the oral surgeon and continues reading in the reception room? Bad luck! In today's publishing world, those reviews would probably mean the death of those books and perhaps the disappearance of those authors.

It gets even worse. As thoughtful a critic as John Updike ("I became a reviewer in part to assuage my sense of indignation about some of the reviews I've got, so that I would sort of show what a fair review should be") has catalogued how his personal feelings of the moment sometimes seasoned his reviews: "Here and there filial affection for an older writer has pulled my punch. Fear of reprisal may have forced a grin or two . . . In other cases irritations of the moment added their personal pepper." A review he did of Dostoevsky was composed "during a mysterious attack of tendonitis; I could not sleep, and sat up all night, watching dawn infiltrate Menemsha Bight, my throbbing left wrist held above my head while my right hand confidently advised Dostoevsky to keep trying."[55] What if Updike was assigned a first novel to review and had another attack of tendonitis as he read the book and wrote his review? If Dostoevsky came up short, who wouldn't?

"Tis the good reader that makes the good book," Emerson said. It's not as if Updike and Porter, Capote and Vidal, and, for that matter, probably most critics, are not good readers. The question is, what are these readers bringing to the book at that moment they review it? Thus, the author whose book has been sent out to be reviewed sees his pages riffled by the fickle hand of fate.

Books can be medicines for the soul; but if medicines made their way to the ill the same way that books made their way to the reader, human civilization would have been wiped out long ago by epidemics of typhus and cholera. For what are critics but the Food and Drug Administration for readers, telling the stores what to stock, telling us what is good for us and what is not? The big difference is that the

FDA has developed a very structured screening process for bringing new drugs to market, whereas a critic may be you, or me, or that troglodyte down the street who may say anything he pleases about the book he reviews.

(Those troglodytes down the street have a new sandbox in which to play with the reader reviews anyone -- and that means anyone! — may post on Amazon: "the worst book I ever read;" "A real bore;" "Didn't care for the writing style." Well, thank you very much. How enlightening. Here are some recent classic ones on classics: —

To Kill A Mockingbird:

"I read more than half of it . . . but at last I had to set it down and accept that I really did not connect with any of the characters in this book at all. To me, this book was drawn out, dry, a waste of my time. I would not recommend it to anyone."

"It was terrible. I don't like it at all. I was so bored and stressed reading this awful book. Ugh."

The Great Gatsby:

"Fitzgerald's words leave me scratching my head wondering 'What is he trying to say?'"

"*The Great Gatsby* has neither enjoyment nor meaning, despite what all the critics and analysts may think." (This "reader" grades it a C-.)

"It was like trying to swallow terrible tasting medicine."

"As boring today as it was in 1925."

The Catcher in the Rye:

"THE most dull, boaring [sic], cringe-worthy book I've ever had to force myself to read. Pure torture & a massive waste of time."

"This book is unequivocal trash."

"This book itself is a tedious read. Dull, long-winded and repetitive, Caulfield rambles aimlessly through what is supposed to be a couple of days but reads like 10 years."

(Exactly who are these anonymous "readers"? One can at least research what else they have reviewed. And find that invariably, every one of them seem to have written effusive poetic praises, and assigned the highest Amazon rating of "5," to their weekly purchase of a 32 fl. oz. bottle of Astroglide.)

The foremost purpose of professional criticism should be to give books the readership they deserve, for a book unread is a book that doesn't exist. As Henry Seidel Canby, the former chairman of the board of judges of the Book-of-the Month Club, said, "The primary object of all writing about books, we take it, is to give them currency. For the best book in the world is worth nothing at all if it never finds a reader."[56] "Better to praise and share than blame and bury,"[57] is the way John Updike put it.

Reviewers who have authored books understand this. Anthony Burgess once said, "In my capacity as critic I never stab anybody, for I know how life-denying it is to be stabbed. Writing a book is damned difficult work, and you ought to praise a book if you can." This opinion was shared by Kurt Vonnegut: "I have long felt that

any reviewer who expresses rage and loathing for a novel is prepos-
terous. He or she is like a person who has just put on full armor and
attacked a hot fudge sundae or banana split."[58] James Atlas, an editor
of the *New York Times Magazine*, dished out his share of nasty reviews until his novel was banged up a bit, at which time he made a
vow: He would still tell the truth about a book, but he would tell it
"in a gingerly way and with genuine remorse," because, he explained,
"they think we can take it, but we can't."[59] And John Irving:

> I write only favorable reviews ... If I get a book to review
> and I don't like it, I return it; I only review the book if I
> love it. Hence I've written very few reviews, and those are
> really just songs of praise or rather long, retrospective re-
> views of all the writer's works ... Another thing about not
> writing negative reviews: grown-ups shouldn't finish books
> they're not enjoying. When you're no longer a child, and you
> no longer live at home, you don't have to finish everything
> on your plate. One reward of leaving school is that you don't
> have to finish books you don't like. You know, if I were a
> critic, I'd be angry and vicious, too; it *makes* poor critics an-
> gry and vicious – to have to *finish* all those books they're not
> enjoying. What a silly job criticism is! What unnatural work
> it is! It is certainly not work for a grown-up![60]

So read that book, reviewer. Read it like a reader. What was the
author trying to do? How close did he come to succeeding in what
he attempted? Quote from the book to support your assessment.
Where are you, the critic, coming from? Within what framework
are you reading and analyzing the book? Did you like it? What did
you like? What didn't you like? If you have a predisposition against
a book, don't review it. (A major review in the *New Times Book Review* of Anais Nin's diary, *A Journal of Love*, began: "My idea of hell
is to be stranded on a desert island with nothing to read but Anais

Nin's dairies, but some people, apparently, can't get enough of them. Her publishers, for instance."[61] That's just silly. How did the *Times* pick this reviewer? Why didn't the reviewer disqualify herself? Why did she bother to write this review? Why did the *Times* publish it?)

Ask yourself: Who would like this book? Who wouldn't like the book? Is your review free of ridicule, disparagement, prophetic pronouncements from Olympus? Be interesting, be entertaining, certainly; but being clever, being cute, is not the role of the critic. John Steinbeck claimed he knew critics "who, thinking up a wise crack — wait happily for a book to come along to apply it to. This is creativeness — not criticism."[62] Telling what a book is about; telling who would, or would not, like it; describing why the author succeeds or does not succeed in what he has attempted to do: this is criticism.

"Literature" said Jules Renard, "is an occupation in which you have to keep proving your talent to people who have none."[63] As satisfying a thought as this might be, it does not convey the real problem. These are not people without talent, these people who mistakenly reject manuscripts or who write rotten reviews. The real problem is that the manuscript, or the completed book, by chance has fallen into the wrong hands — the hands, for instance, of a William Styron, who, as an editorial assistant at McGraw Hill, rejected *Kon-Tiki*, helpfully suggesting it might be suitable for a magazine article; or the hands of a publisher or reviewer who, at that point in his or her life, does not really understand a book like *The Catcher in the Rye*, when a colleague down the hall might be a parent with a Holden at home.

When the review copies are sent out a month or six weeks before publication date, the author had better cross his fingers tightly and pray for a run of luck, for at that point he has stepped up to the table and said to the croupier: put it all — the blood, toil, sweat and tears of the last several years of my life — put it all on twenty- seven.

JACQUELINE SUSANN: PATRON SAINT OF WRITERS?

AUTHORS MAY KEEP A SHINY HORSE CHESTNUT and worn rabbit's foot in their pockets (Ernest Hemingway), and make sure they never stop writing on page thirteen or a multiple of thirteen (Stephen King), but the luck necessary to turn a book into a best-selling book cannot be coaxed. It comes when it damn well pleases.

There's one author, though, who grabbed luck by the short hairs and pulled it out of hiding, and she, Jackie Susann, deserves to be the Patron Saint of Writers.

Jacqueline Susann? Yes.

That tough broad who Truman Capote said looked "like a truck driver in drag"?[1] That's the one.

The one about whom Gore Vidal quipped, "she doesn't write, she types"?[2]

Right.

The one who wrote all that dreck, those trashy novels about drugs and sex and scandal? Precisely.

Jacqueline Susann? You bet.

That tough broad who, as it turned out, was of course not as tough as she pretended, suffered every defeat, every humiliation, every indignity the publishing world has to dish out, and then turned right around and kicked some publishing butt. She caught everyone's attention.

SCENE I

Jackie Bangs at the Locked Door of Publishing

What was Jackie's first book? No, not *Valley of the Dolls*. No, it wasn't *Every Night, Josephine*, the story about her French poodle. For a dozen years she had been trying her hand at plays and books, each of which was rejected. She was no young success who burst upon the scene. She had known all the anguish and frustration of trying to break into print. Her writing was going nowhere, and her dreams of an acting career, her years of bit parts (she was often cast as a murderess or murder victim) were pretty much over in 1962 when, at the age of forty-four, she was diagnosed with breast cancer. She later revealed she bargained with God: Just give me ten more years, ten years to prove I'm the writer I think I am.

SCENE II

Jackie Is Humiliated by the Publishing World

Jacqueline Susann signed a contract with Doubleday for the publication of *Every Night, Josephine*. (Can't you just hear her telephoning all her friends: I've written a book and it's being published. By Doubleday! Yes! Doubleday!) But to her disbelief, she discovered that the book contract had no fixed publication date and that Doubleday would not publish her book until another dog book that was under contract had been completed and published. Jackie's husband — television producer, agent, and hustler Irving Mansfield — was furious and pulled the book back from Doubleday. Jackie, according to Mansfield, "had a fit." "But I've told all my friends that Doubleday is publishing my book! What will I tell them now? They'll think I lied to them!"[3]

As always, Irving knew just what a book needed, and brought his wife's manuscript to Bernard Geis Associates, a new publishing house.

Bernard Geis had been the editor at Prentice Hall who worked on Art Linkletter's book, *Kids Say the Darndest Things*, which came out in 1957. Linkletter, who constantly promoted the book on his TV show, was so taken by its rise to the top of the nonfiction best-seller lists, where it lodged for a year, that he backed Geis in starting his own publishing house. That house would devote itself exclusively to the publication of ten or twelve books each year, books that could be promoted on television, that is, books that had the potential to be promoted into best- sellers. As Geis explained it, his publishing house was founded on the premise "that books are underpromoted and undermerchandized — the distribution of trade books is moribund. I can take any book, Stendhal or Max Shulman, and double or triple its sale by exposing it to the mass media."[4] Added Geis's director of promotion: "Our authors can rest assured we'll do our part. Other publishers live in an ivory tower. They think mass communications are a nasty business. But the rest of the world is watching TV. It's not enough to seek the habitual book buyers, a few thousand urban sophisticates. We reach out to the people who read gossip columns and women's pages. We present the author as a celebrity in her own right."[5] Helen Gurley Brown's *Sex and the Single Girl* was one of Geis's best-sellers.

SCENE III

Jackie Sets Off on the Tour from Hell

Bernard Geis Associates might have been headed in an interesting direction, but it still had a lot to learn. Jackie's first publicity tour was a disaster.

On the West Coast, only one television show had been booked, and that show wanted Jackie only if her dog was with her; Josephine was back home in New York. No Josephine, no Jackie.

The Mansfields checked out the local bookstores and found not a single copy of *Every Night, Josephine*, nor a bookstore manager who had even heard of it.

Mansfield concluded that the book business "must be a pretty funny business to mess up on getting books and announcements to bookstores."[6]

In Chicago, Jackie had an interview on what her husband called a "five-watt radio station." "I think maybe four people heard the interview," Mansfield complained. "It cost us thirty dollars by taxi each way."[7]

When, through her husband's own promotional efforts, carried out with his own cash, the book began to get some publicity and sneaked onto a regional best- seller list or two, Jackie happened to learn the good news not from her publisher, but while browsing through a magazine.

SCENE IV

Jackie Confronts the Opacity of the Publishing World

For her next book, *Valley of the Dolls*, Jackie received (now mind you, her previous book had indeed grazed some best-seller lists) the munificent stipend of $3,000. So much for the loyal support of a publisher. The first readers of *Valley of Dolls* at Bernard Geis Associates pleaded with Bernie Geis to drop it and run. "You've already invested three thousand dollars in an advance on this book. Don't throw good money after bad. It's literary trash." "*Valley of the Dolls* was hardly written in English," another of Geis's editors sighed. "She is a painfully dull, inept, clumsy, undisciplined, rambling and thoroughly amateurish writer whose every sentence, paragraph and scene cries for the hand of a pro . . . I really don't think there is a page of this ms. that can stand in its present form."[8] So much for the perspicacity of the editors of the one publishing house in the United States devoted solely to making best-sellers.

When the bids for a paperback reprint of *Valley of the Dolls* were due (before the hardcover publication), there was a distressing, numbing silence. Not one had been submitted. At the last moment, at Bernard Geis's personal prodding, Bantam put in an insignificant bid that discouraged Susann and her publisher alike. Geis reported the bid to other paperback houses to see if some action could be stirred up, to no avail. Geis then went back to Bantam and implied that there were other bids and that to get the book it would have to raise its offer, which it did.

As it turned out, Bantam need not have been upset about being taken for a ride. That bid proved to be quite a bargain when *Valley of the Dolls* became the fastest paperback seller of all times, with eight million copies sold in seven months. But Bantam's bid had not been based on its insight into the potential of the book; Bantam's was a clouded vision shared by the professionals at the host of other paperback houses to which the book had been submitted. Not one book club bid on the book.

SCENE V

Jackie Is Panned by the Critics

To the extent she received reviews at all, Susann's novels were trashed. Gloria Steinem concluded that "for the reader who has put away comic books but isn't yet ready for editorials in the *Daily News*, V.O.T.D. may bridge an awkward gap."[9] Later, Christopher Lehmann-Haupt of the *New York Times* called her next novel, *The*

Love Machine, "popcorn." "It goes down quickly and easily. It is the kernel of an idea, the seed of an inspiration, exploded into bite-sized nothingness."[10] "Once is more than enough, as this book, and all of Jacqueline Susann's books prove," the *New York Times* review of *Once Is Not Enough* quite predictably began. *Time* dismissed it as "the dirty book of the month."[11]

SCENE VI

Who the Hell Cares?

Jackie and Irving were very quick studies; or maybe, knowing that Jackie's time was short, were ready to work harder and faster and longer than anyone else. Whatever it was, neither their publisher's ineptitude, nor the discouraging reviews, nor the lack of interest of the paperback houses and book clubs and national television shows bothered them one bit. Takeoff time, T minus 1, was at hand.

Off went fifteen hundred free copies of *Valley of the Dolls* — at that time an extraordinary number — to anyone, anywhere, who might help publicize the book.

Off went Jackie and Irving, right behind them. Together, Jackie and Irving carefully plotted how to promote Jackie's new book. The staid world of book publishing was outdated, archaic, they concluded. "Usually all they ever do to help an author is give a little luncheon attended by two or three editors including one from the New York Times who perspires too much," Jackie remarked. "It seemed to me that if I'd spent eighteen months writing the book the least I could do was spend three months promoting it."[12]

Those three months turned into twelve as the Mansfields, at their own expense, traveled the country, back and forth, again and again, for Jackie to appear on national and local television shows, at bookstores and for newspaper and radio interviews Irving had lined up. In each city, they hired a taxi and made the rounds of all the bookstores, talking to the manager and clerks, making sure *Valley of the Dolls* was prominently displayed. Because Jackie and Irving cared, the bookstores cared and helped promote the book. When Jackie found a bookstore clerk with the brass to admit he hadn't read her book, she bought him a copy, paid for it, and autographed it for him. "A clerk won't really push a book if he hasn't read it himself," she explained.[13] Each bookdealer was given an autographed photograph of himself with Jackie; another copy was sent to his local newspaper. She wrote personal notes to each bookstore owner, to everyone who had helped her or been nice to her on her tour, each with a personal anecdote. She kept a card file on bookstore clerks and knew their first names, intentionally cultivating friendships with owners of bookstores across the country to the point where some of them indeed numbered among her closest friends.

The Mansfields visited the book distributors at four o'clock in the morning as the books were being loaded onto trucks, bringing them coffee and Danish, talking to the drivers, giving them autographed copies of her book. What a great idea! What a great copy! The newspapers ate it up as much as the truck drivers.

It was Irving Mansfield who thought of advertising *Valley of the Dolls* in the entertainment pages as well as in a newspapers' book review sections, a successful stratagem that had never before been tried, or apparently even contemplated, a plan that helped the book reach a new group of readers.

Jackie recalled how, in the beginning, none of the television shows had wanted to have her; how her publicist had "threatened, cajoled and begged" to get her a spot on a late night radio show; how she had gotten on Merv Griffin's show only because he was a friend; and how what she accomplished had been done without the benefit of national television. "Almost every city has its own version of *Today*. At that time, there were Roger Grimsby and the late Gypsy Rose Lee

in San Francisco, Regis Philbin in San Diego, Marie Torre in Pitts-
burgh, Tom Snyder in Philadelphia, Irv Kupcinet in Chicago. If you
were willing to travel, you got on. I traveled! I made the list without *Today*, without the *Tonight Show*. I kept 'touring.' I went to De-
troit, Cincinnati, Dallas, Houston. I developed sciatica from sitting
on planes."[14] Although Jacqueline Susann once said that plugging
books on the talk show circuit "ought to rate combat pay,"[15] it must
be remembered that Jackie was not just any old writer appearing on
television. In addition to a husband who had been a television producer and who had the industry contacts, and the chutzpa to use
them and then some, raven-haired Jackie, with her perfect tan and
sparkling capped teeth, had great stage presence, and a sexy smoker's
voice to boot. She had been an actress and now was relishing her
leading role. She had the ability, the knack, the stamina, for giving
six or more interviews a day, enthusiastically answering the same
questions time and again, day after day, appearing on one hundred
television shows and two hundred radio shows to promote *Valley of
the Dolls* (Bernard Geis once commented that "someone said then
the only thing you could turn on without getting Jacqueline Susann
was the water faucet"[16]), adeptly returning any straying interviewer
to the only important topic: her book. She was clever enough not to
talk directly about the plot of *Valley of the Dolls*, but rather, for example, the abuse of pills by the rich and famous. As Geis noted, "She
would *deny* that her characters were based on celebrities. She would
deny that the one character was really modelled on Judy Garland.
She would *deny* that it was really Ethel Merman she was portraying in
the book."[17] With each denial, the resulting rumors and speculation
flamed more interest in *Valley of the Dolls*.

Jackie was comfortable and relaxed enough before a camera to
have some fun, which guaranteed return appearances.

When her novel, *The Love Machine*, and Philip Roth's *Portnoy's
Complaint* were vying for the top position on the fiction best-seller

lists, she commented about Roth: "I like the book but I'd hate to shake his hand,"[18] adding in another interview that "Philip Roth's started a 'do-it-yourself club' and that it had taken him so long to write the novel because 'he could only type with one hand.'"[19]

On the David Frost show, critic John Simon asked her, "Do you think you are writing art or are you writing trash to make a lot of money?"

"Little man," she snapped, "I am telling a story. Now does that make you happy?"[20]

An interviewer asked her, "Don't you ever wake up in the middle of the night and realize you haven't done anything that is really artistic?"

"You're sick," Jackie shot back. "Do you wake up and think you're not Huntley-Brinkley?"[21]

When one interviewer asked, "What do you think is the reason for everybody reading your book, apart from the obvious?" Jackie responded with a question of her own: "What's the obvious reason?"

"Sex, pure and simple," answered the interviewer.

No, Jackie responded, it was not sex that sold her books. "I'm a today writer. The novel today has to compete with television and the movies. It has to come alive quickly and be easy to read. When people tell you they couldn't put the book down, that is good writing."[22]

Jackie's editor remarked once that "Jackie and Irving were the most phenomenal, tenacious, successful, innovative, and inventive book promoters who ever lived. With Jackie and Irving there was no limit. They called in every IOU they had and pulled every trick they knew."[23] These tricks included a book buying campaign described by Jackie's biographer, Barbara Seadman, in *Lovely Me*:

> Clearly *Valley's* momentum was largely due to the publicity. However, there was a second factor that inflated the early sales: a book-buying campaign apparently orchestrated by

Irving and possibly financed in part by Bantam and Twentieth Century-Fox, both of which had much to gain if the book could be made a success ... Exactly how buyers in key cities were recruited and financed remains a secret. However, Letty Pogebrin [Geis's director of publicity] says that in those days the names of the specific bookstores reporting to the list were "common knowledge."[24]

It would not be surprising if Irving had indeed been able to shake down Bantam, which had bought the paperback rights, and Twentieth Century-Fox, which had bought the movie rights, to contribute funds to keep the book at the top of the lists for as long as possible. "If anyone tells you that publishing is a gentleman's profession," he once scoffed, "I suggest you just laugh."[25]

Jackie and Irving's relentless work got the momentum going, and going, and going, until sales of *Valley of the Dolls* jumped from a few hundred copies a week to over six thousand weekly, peaking at 8,500 a day. On the best-seller lists for sixty-two weeks, *Valley of the Dolls* eventually sold over 30 million copies in hardcover and paperback, was purchased by more people than any other American novel of the twentieth century, and according to the *Guinness Book of World Records*, is the best-selling novel of all time.

"Money is applause," the actress turned novelist said.[26] The applause she had never known in her acting career was bringing down the house in her writing career. "The biggest thing of all," Jacqueline Susann believed, "is *being* Number One, being on top of that list that's in every bookstore." She went on:

People just look at the list and buy the book. It's the in thing to do. And when a book hits a hundred thousand, it will do two hundred thousand because now you're reaching people who rarely buy books. At ninety thousand you've hit all the people who go to Brentano's and Doubleday; over that you're getting people who buy in department stores and discount houses. Men buy mostly nonfiction, history, biography. But if a book has that extra thing, if it's a real story, if it's excitement, then men will buy it, if it's only to find out why their wives sit up with it all night. And when that happens, the book will just sail, and nobody can stop it, critics, nobody.[27]

She would follow *Valley of the Dolls* with two more number one best-selling novels, *The Love Machine* and *Once Is Not Enough*. "If I knew what made a best- seller," Jacqueline Susann commented as *The Love Machine* was just coming out with an advance sale of 200,000 (which quickly climbed to 300,000 copies in print a week later, and which had just received a million dollar bid for the movie rights), "I wouldn't sweat and stalk beaches, parks and the zoo when I get hung up with my writing."[28] But she had a pretty good clue.

Jackie's editor of *The Love Machine* at Simon & Schuster, Michael Korda, believed that Jackie's promotional skills were the key to her success. Without them, he was convinced, the book would probably have sold about 100,000 copies, "but it wouldn't have the great impact it does. Jackie has succeeded where no one has before in tapping all the modern means of communication in one great campaign – movies, television, newspaper interviews, magazines, commercials, all cleverly bound together."[29]

This was Simon & Schuster's first entry into the brave new world of commercial fiction. "Just turn it into a book somehow, that's all I ask," were the first instructions editor Michael Korda was given by his boss when he reported that the manuscript was all but incoherent. That proved to be the easiest part of the work. The publishing house, accustomed to launching a big book with a sedate cocktail party and a spot for the author on *The Today Show*, found itself throwing lavish parties on both coasts, sending out thousands of gift ankhs in presentation cases shaped like books, devising posters, displays, cakes in the shape of a book: There was no end to Jackie's ideas, her requests, her demands. Not satisfied with Simon & Schuster's performance, Jackie switched to William Morrow for her next book. The head of Simon & Schuster sent her a single rose on the publication date of *Once is Not Enough*, with a note: "For us, once *was* enough."[30]

It was only with the recurrence of cancer in 1972 that Jackie began cutting back her typical twenty-nine talk shows and newspaper interviews a week, a diminution of activity which worried her no end: "Even a good book can die on the vine if it's not promoted."[31]

Jackie's publishers hadn't learned all the lessons she had tried to teach, though other authors had. Less than two years after Jackie's death in 1974, agent Morton Janklow brought to Simon & Schuster the first novel of one of his new authors, Judith Krantz. It was called *Scruples* and was about the sex and scandal of the super rich of Beverly Hills' Rodeo Drive. Simon & Schuster turned it down, as Judith Krantz remembered, "because they didn't like it."[32] Crown Publishers did like it and brought it out in March of 1978, at which time it soared to the top of the *New York Times* Best Sellers list and stayed on the list for about a year, selling over a million copies in hardcover.

Perhaps Simon & Schuster had not learned to recognize the winning formula of Jackie Susann that Judith Krantz applied to her book. Or perhaps the publisher did not recognize in Judith Krantz the same drive, the same marketability, that Jackie Susann had possessed. Off went Judith Krantz, crossing the country to appear on every television and radio show, at every bookstore and women's club that would have her, cultivating the booksellers, bubbling effervescently about her book. "I never realized before how much hustling was involved," she said after the completion of her hardcover tour and before she set off on her paperback tour. "Touring for a book — it's the literary equivalent of war."[33]

Harvey Mackay is another example of an author who followed in Jacqueline Susann's footsteps. The Minneapolis businessman was running an envelope company when he wrote *Swim with the Sharks*

Without Being Eaten Alive, a title picked by a consulting firm which, for $5,000, tested it in the market against hundreds of others. That's indicative of how this businessman approached his first book. It wasn't just money he had to spend; it was also a lot of aggressiveness and a phenomenal sales technique.

Before he began writing his book, MacKay visited over one hundred bookstores across the country and talked with more than one hundred authors, reaching the conclusion that most books fail simply because they are not available in the stores. That would not happen to him. He persuaded his publisher, William Morrow & Company, to do an initial run of 100,000 copies by promising to pay the cost of a twenty-six city promotional tour. He persuaded forty-three Names, of the likes of Mario Cuomo, Gerald Ford, Ted Koppel and Robert Redford, to write blurbs for his book. At the Frankfurt Book Fair, which his publishers had discouraged him from attending, he sold the rights to his book to thirty foreign publishers. At each of the twenty-six cities he visited, he stopped in at dozens of bookstores, showing the owners how best to display his book. Need it be added that *Swim with the Sharks Without Being Eaten Alive* stayed on the best-seller lists for thirty-six weeks? It was Jackie's winning formula, carried out to perfection.

These stories of Jacqueline Susann and Judith Krantz and Harvery MacKay; of Thomas A. Harris, whose book, *I'm OK, You're OK*, had meager first year sales, but who didn't give up, giving talks to small audiences and stirring up enough sales that his publishers launched a first rate promotional campaign, resulting ultimately in sales of over one million copies; of Dr. Wayne W. Dyer, who packed 400 copies of his *Your Erroneous Zones* into the trunk of his car and set off, traveling around the country, talking with local newspaper-men and on local radio stations, with his book thereafter making the best-seller lists: These stories of the triumph of authors over the system are heartwarming indeed. But beware their Circean seduction. It doesn't always work out that way. It's like what Annie Dillard said in *The Writing Life* about how long it takes to write a book: two to ten years for most authors, she posits, qualifying her statement by noting that "out of a human population on earth of four and a half billion, perhaps twenty people can write a book in a year. Some people lift cars, too . . . There is no call to take human extremes as norm."[34] The Susanns and the Krantzes and the MacKays of the world are the car-lifters, those very unique individuals who can successfully promote a book themselves. It's not easy.

Jacqueline Susann: Patron Saint of Writers.

Not because her novels were literary masterpieces.

Not because *Valley of the Dolls* holds the record as the fastest paperback seller of all times or because it was purchased by more people than any other American novel of the twentieth century.

Not because of her succession of number one hits.

And not because Jackie established a road map for others to follow in promoting books; few authors have the special personality, the resources, the stamina to replicate what she accomplished.

What Jacqueline Susann showed is that the more attention and time an author and publisher devote to the promotion of a book, the more likely it is that the book will achieve the sales it deserves. She showed that it is not enough just to toss a newly-published book out into the world to see what will happen, and then to sigh, "Those are the breaks," when the inevitable nothing happens. As Michael Korda has said, "Jackie and Irving taught me that books can be merchandised, just like anything else – something that a lot of publishers have yet to learn. Today, she is a prophet without honor, but John Grisham, Robert James Waller, Judith Krantz, Jackie Collins, Danielle Steel and the rest all owe her a debt."

Jacqueline Susann proved that the sales success of a book can be made. Hats off to Jackie!

"MY HUCKLEBERRY FRIEN

Encounters with Gloria Van,

IT ALL BEGAN JUST THE WAY GLORIA LATER WOULD TELL ME all magical parts of our lives begin: there would be a knock on the door, the phone would ring, a letter would arrive, and just like that, our lives would change forever.

My book, *Gardening in Eden*, had been published in 2003. I liked it a lot, but had spent eighteen months trying to find a publisher who agreed with my favorable assessment. For a year and a half, the largest commercial publishing houses, to the pathetically puniest boutiques, had summarily rejected it with nary a scribbled "not bad" on one of their form rejection letters, when I received a phone call at the office from Michael Korda, the editor-in-chief of Simon & Schuster, telling me he'd love to publish it and would be my editor. In abject gratitude for his perspicacity, I dedicated the book to him. We received a glowing bouquet of blurbs for the dust jacket, but that was about it, for the book on publication fell flat on its face, with no reviews, and sales as anemic as a scraggly impatiens. Any friends who even referred to its existence invariably said that they were "not really into gardening" so had not read it, yet, though my book had about as much to do with how-to-garden as *Walden* had to do with how-to-construct a cabin in the woods.

So when I got home from work one day that Spring and found in the mail a letter from a reader saying how much my book had meant to her, I soaked up the praise as the parched soil around that scraggly impatiens would soak up the rain. And because that reader, and that letter writer, was Gloria Vanderbilt, I read it again and again, absorbing the nourishing rain through every pore.

ARTHUR T. VANDERBILT II

never met Gloria, never corresponded with her, and, being
om a different branch of the family, felt no connection to her. Yet
here was one of the most iconic, recognized women of the twentieth
century, writing to me, telling me about how much she enjoyed my
book and, how much she would love to come see my garden.

About fifteen years before, I had written *Fortune's Children: The Fall of the House of Vanderbilt*, and a section of that book had dealt with the famous custody battle for ten year old Gloria Vanderbilt, a ferocious battle between two momma bears, her very young globe-trotting mother, Gloria, and her very wealthy aunt, Gertrude Vanderbilt Whitney. Talk about a headline case: this custody battle and the trial in "Matter of Vanderbilt" were daily front page news in 1934 during those dark days of the Depression. Having read about her abhorrence to talking about her past, and her constant refusals to be interviewed about it, I had not even tried to reach out to her when I was researching and writing my book. Now, here was a character right from its pages, writing to me, saying how much she would like to come visit. It was as if Samuel Clemens answered his doorbell and saw Tom Sawyer standing there, looking at him.

I of course wrote back. I always answered each of the reader letters I received, which was not so hard to do since rare was the month when I received as many as one. And thanked her for her kind words and said I'd love to show her the garden, any time, believing that would be that. By return mail, Gloria replied: when? when might be a convenient time?

Lord, was she serious about this? She was. As I read her reply and this began to sink in, I was sweating. Now, I've had a lot of fun with my garden and to me it is a work of art, but I was not quite so deluded that I believed it anything more than an amateur's effort, that someone like Gloria Vanderbilt had seen all the great gardens of the world, and what I had done on my shy half acre was not worth her time. I pictured her getting out of a stretch limo, taking one look

144

at where she was, and saying "Oh ...," the same sort of "Oh ..." I had heard in every form rejection letter.

I responded with a date, sure her social calendar would be filled. Her response, "Perfect!," was in the return mail.

How do you transport a world-famous eighty-year old heiress from New York City into the wilds of New Jersey? I offered to line up a driver for her, sure she would say that Beasley would be driving her. (Beasley had been her mother's chauffeur before the child custody trial in the 1930s, so maybe it would be Beasley's son, or grandson, or a Beasley equivalent?) "That would be lovely" came her reply.

What do you do to prepare for the arrival of such a guest? You can be sure that in the remaining days every leaf in my garden was hand-polished, every blade of grass precision cut, every brick in the paths scrubbed. For a week, daily sacrifices and offerings were made to the weather gods that the big day would be sunny and fair.

And it was. As the hour approached, I had no idea what to expect, what to say. I visualized the arrival of a diva, bedecked in jewels. When the Lincoln Town car arrived and the driver opened the back door, out stepped Gloria, in a very simple cotton dress and straw hat and sandals, no tiara, no jewelry, not even a ring on a finger.

Here was one of the most famous women of her time, in the headlines since birth — first as a baby in a fabled family, at that time the richest in the world, then for the custody battle, later for her many affairs and four marriages, someone photographed at every opening night, at every charity event, perennially on the best dressed lists, famous for her Vanderbilt jeans, her television ads featuring her perfect butt and wispy WASPy voice, her perfumes, her fashion empire. And the first thing I blurted out was "Oh my God! Its Anderson Cooper's mother!"

She smiled. Her smile, like Gatsby's, had "a quality of eternal reassurance in it," but behind it she seemed as shy, as fragile, as Laura in *The Glass Menagerie*, as if it had taken as much courage for her to reach out to come visit a stranger as it did for me to welcome a celebrity into my home. She seemed so vulnerable that every instinct to protect her came to the fore.

She stood looking at me for a moment: "oh, yes," she said quietly. Though not a direct descendent in her family line, some of the Vanderbilt genes must be so dominant that I do bear a striking resemblance to many of her forebears whose portraits hang in The Breakers. That, and my mention that we shared the same birth date – February 20 – and it was as if we had known each other and been friends for life. We began calling each other "cousin."

I lead our tour out through the French doors in the sunroom to the terrace, and, babbling away, up the stone steps that lead to the garden paths, all the while silently praying that a neighbor won't choose that moment to start mowing their lawn or using a cyclonic leaf blower. But all was quiet save the rustle of the new green leaves of the oaks and the chirping of happy birds, straight out of a Disney film, when I realized I had lost my tour. I looked back. Gloria was standing in front of the large green nineteenth century demijohn I had filled with water and placed on the brick wall around the terrace garden, standing back, pacing around it, examining it from every angle. I walked back to her.

"Enchanting," she whispered reverently, as if examining the Hope Diamond. "This is exquisite."

I explained that my grandmother had had it on the wall around her sunken garden in Maine and I had always been taken by the color, the way the sunlight passed through the green, illuminating it like a stained glass window.

"Enchanting," Gloria said again, and showed no signs of wanting to move on. She was committing it to memory, and I realized later she would have liked to have sketched it, to have sat right there and painted it, for she was looking at the world with an artist's eye and a child's sense of wonder, how everything to her, even in this, her eightieth Spring, was new and fresh as if never seen before, as if this was the world's first day. This green bottle had enchanted me since the time I was a child but this was the first time I had met anyone who had shared my fascination.

"There's more," I promised, trying to lure her onward. At the rate we were moving, it would be dark before we left for dinner.

Gloria was the kind of guest gardeners fantasize about as we're on our hands and knees trying to pry an impacted rock out of a hole to plant a hosta, or battling slugs and groundhogs, or nuking weeds, someone who sees our garden as we see it in our mind's eye, something that matches the images and fantasies in our dreams that we try, always unsuccessfully, to bring to life.

I led her along the brick paths, past drifts of Virginia bluebells and violets and Johnny Jump-Ups and Jack-in-the-Pulpits and red tulips, islands of hosta, moss and lichen covered statues of the four seasons looking so old that they may have been lifted from a Renaissance garden, a peek into the gazebo with its small glass-topped table and two chairs that would have been perfect for a Parisian café, to a hidden nook with a long weathered teak bench surrounded by arbor vita and forsythia, with the oaks and ash towering over it.

"Oh, my," Gloria said, as if entering a fairytale forest. "Let's sit down here so that I may remember this."

We sat. And she put her hand in mine.

I was holding the hand that had held the hand of Marlon Brando. Of Howard Hughes. Of Frank Sinatra. Of Truman Capote. Of Bobby Short. Of Anderson Cooper. The thought of which might have been enough to turn my hand into a raging river of sweat. But with Gloria, we were transported into a Zen state, inhaling the green of Spring, listening to the music of birds, hearing what the rustle of the oak leaves was trying to tell us. And it was a long time before either of us broke the silence of that dreamy afternoon.

Never before, or since, have I encountered anyone with such a deep appreciation of life, of being alive, of the miraculous wonder of the moment.

There was about an hour to kill before we would leave for dinner and now we sat in the sunroom, talking. Gloria assumed I knew all about her financial problems, which had been in the news some years before, but I didn't, the story of how, after the sudden death of her husband Wyatt Cooper at the age of fifty, and the suicide of her twenty-year old son Carter who fell to his death from her penthouse terrace as she begged him to stop, she had begun to see a psychiatrist, who, in her vulnerable state, eventually took financial advantage of her, having her sign over to him — unknowingly — the keys to her fashion empire, leaving her with enormous tax liabilities and no income. I gathered, in asking a few gentle questions, she was having serious trouble making ends meet on a monthly basis, it was that bad. I sensed she would never trouble her famous son, Anderson, with her problems.

We began brainstorming ideas for making a come-back in the fashion industry; she was game, but different avenues all seemed blocked by whatever she had signed. I then moved on, encouraging her to write a book. Some years before she had written two about her early years, *Once Upon a Time*, and *Black Knight, White Knight*, both of which had been well received and bestsellers. Why not one about her friendship with Truman Capote? She visibly cringed. "I would never do anything to keep his name alive," she hissed. And snarled. I knew that while they had been best friends, the friendship ended when he published *Answered Prayers* with its cruel depictions of Gloria and some of her friends, but I hadn't realized how deep her dislike of him still ran, decades later. Okay, scratch that idea. How about portraits of some of the famous people she had known, and I mentioned a handful. I could see her turning this idea over

148

in her mind, and the fact that she didn't dismiss it summarily perhaps meant that it may have taken root.

I took her to dinner at nearby Baltusrol Golf Club where we sat at a corner table, looking out over the perfect green course and lovely pond as the evening darkened. There, Gloria did something I was to observe time and again: she all but vanished in front of my eyes, doing nothing to call attention to herself, melting into anonymity. As eager as my eyes were to dart about, flashing in neon an SOS: "Look Who is Sitting With Me!," I protected her privacy. Part way through the dinner, Bill, the bartender who had been there over fifty years and had met everyone, from the Duke of Windsor to Arnold Palmer to Dwight Eisenhower, came over and very quietly said "Good evening, Mrs. Vanderbilt" as if it was the most natural thing in the world, just the way Scout said "Hey Boo" in that final scene of *To Kill a Mockingbird*. And Gloria said hello as quietly, as shyly, as Boo.

When we finished dessert — by now we were laughing because we were finding how similar we were, we both had ordered the same appetizers, the same main course and for dessert rice pudding, our favorite — the driver I had arranged was at the front door to take Gloria back to the City. We embraced and waved goodbye. Which I assumed would be forever.

Except that when I awoke and checked my computer — we had exchanged email addresses — there was a note from Gloria that she had sent before dawn, thanking me for her garden tour, and then getting right to the point: "which of these do you like as a title for my book?" listing three or four for the book she said she had decided to write about her "romances."

From that moment on, I was present at creation, with email ideas flying back and forth, often several times a day, and occasionally a draft chapter faxed to me for comments. Gloria was looking to me as her first reader, to offer ideas and criticisms, but her way of writing was so idiosyncratic, her experiences so other-worldly, that to change a word, or to try to re-arrange a thought, felt like disturbing a delicate, perfectly balanced mobile.

Opening the chapters Gloria was faxing to me was like opening treasure chests, never knowing what to expect, but always being dazzled, from her first affair with a prep school friend, to finding a Bible in Truman Capote's bathroom with the pages cut out to form a secret place to hid cocaine, to Howard Hughes flying her to Catalina, being chased around Bill Paleys penthouse in the St. Regis, sleeping with Marlon Brando who was "more more more everything than even I could have possibly imagined," how on the table next to his bed was a ten by twelve "drop- dead-gorgeous-photograph" of himself in a silver frame, Frank Sinatra singing "My Funny Valentine" to her, all wrapped around those dreamlike days to be very young and very beautiful and very rich in old New York before the War.

Gloria titled her manuscript *It Seemed Important at the Time.* I was convinced it would be a bestseller, but, unsure of its merits, Gloria asked what to do next. I suggested she contact Michal Korda, who was pleased to publish with Simon & Schuster. Even then Gloria had little understanding of her celebrity status and how to use it to promote her book. "Get on Oprah." I advised, and when she replied "how would I do that?" as if that was the most impossible thing imaginable. I was dumbfounded, knowing I would have milked that same recognition to promote one of my books. "Just call her and say you'd like to come on to discuss your new book, all about your affairs with Brando and Sinatra and Hughes." She was too modest to pick up the phone or even to suggest this to her publisher's publicity department.

But she did receive invitations to appear here and there, one to come to a major book fair in Scottsdale, Arizona and to be a featured speaker there.

"Would you come with me?" she asked. She could bring one friend. Having guaranteed Gloria that her book would be a best-seller, I was happy to jump into the trenches with her. We planned our three day trip with military precision.

Gloria must have thought I was doing something important at the office because she never called me there, though of course it was my fervent hope that she would. And that I would not be at my desk. And that the receptionist would have to page me: "Mr. Vanderbilt: Please pick up line 9 for Gloria Vanderbilt. Mr. Vanderbilt: Gloria Vanderbilt: line 9." As it turned out, the one time she called — the afternoon before the morning of our flight — I was at my desk. And I was not on the phone. I knew it must be important.

"Oh Art, something terrible has happened," Gloria began in her breathless voice. I braced myself for the worst. "I found out that Scazy will be on our plane!"

She paused dramatically to let the impact of this sink in. "So I had to change our flight."

She waited for my reaction.

I had no idea what she was talking about. What, or who, is a Scazy? A new airborne virus plague? A hijacker? An assassin? An international terrorist intent on blowing up planes? I had missed the Nightly News the evening before; I hadn't yet read the morning paper. What did I miss? I gave what I thought was an appropriately grateful "oh my gosh! Thank goodness you were able to change them!" as I madly googled Scazy.

Scazy? Skasi? Scarsi? Scarzy? Was it a moniker for someone whose face had been cut in a knife fight and was scared? I could see him: nightmarish livid white scars that cut across his cheeks. I shivered. What was she saying? I searched all sorts of combinations, coming up only with Arnold Scaasi who ran a very high- end couture salon in New York City, catering to socialites and celebrities, from Barbra Streisand to Elizabeth Taylor, to Lauren Bacall, Joan Crawford, Brooke Astor, to a host of First Ladies, but no mention at all about any criminal or terrorist proclivities. How did you even spell it? Had I misunderstood what she had said? I wrote down the new flight information she gave me, we would meet at the gate the next morning, 7:15 a.m. "Man we dodged that bullet," I told her as we said goodbye; "Good work!"

I consider myself punctual, some friends would say obsessively so, the rest would say neurotically so, so I arrived at the airport almost an hour before Gloria said to be there, checked my bags and got through security. As I approached our gate, I could see I was way early, there was just one person sitting there, all alone in a chair by the gate.

As always, I had to look closely to be sure. Gloria once again had disappeared in public. As usual there was nothing flashy about her attire. She never looked around. Or even looked up.

I walked over to her.

"Mrs. Vanderbilt, I presume?" I asked.

She looked. "Mr. Vanderbilt. Please have a seat."

We sat and talked as the chairs in the waiting area slowly began to fill with groggy early morning travelers who had no idea who was sitting there with them.

We were deep in conversation, it was almost time to board, when I sensed my space being invaded. Someone was standing in front of us. Much too close. Neither of us looked up. We continued talking.

"Hello, Gloria," the person said.

Gloria looked up and without missing a beat said "Hello Scaasi."

My head jerked back. I stared at him. He didn't look like a terrorist, he didn't look threatening. Was he a stalker who had been served with a restraining order to stay 1,500 feet away from Miss Vanderbilt? He appeared to be in his late sixties, early seventies, wearing a very smart blue blazer with a colorful pocket handkerchief, a striped shirt and very expensive looking silk tie, perfectly pressed gray flannel slacks, and Gucci loafers.

"You are looking very handsome this morning, Arnold," Gloria said.

Scaasi puffed up a little. "Well, you better get used to this outfit because it's all you're going to be seeing for the next few days."

He looked at me, and Gloria introduced us.

"And what do you do," he asked. "Are you a gentleman of leisure?"

Which struck me as quite amusing, as a partner at a law firm where everyone was expected to, had to, bill at least 200 hours a week; not only to physically be there for 200 hours a week, but to have done work that could be billed to clients that would pay for those hours. Try that sometime. It had taken the contortions of a Laocoon to try to arrange my schedule to take three days off.

We said a few words to Scaasi and his partner, Parker Ladd, a distinguished looking gentleman of about the same age, and then they were off into the crowd.

"I can't believe this," Gloria said. "They must have changed their flight just like I did."

Gloria told me she had learned the day before that Scaasi, who had just published a book, *Women I Have Dressed and Undressed*, would be appearing at the same event, which had led her to scramble and shift flights. "I'll tell you later all about him," she said with a roll of her eyes. "At least we're free of them, there will be so many people there. They are expecting thousands, they tell me."

Of course, as fate would have it, Scaasi and Parker had the seats directly across the aisle from us. So Gloria couldn't fill me in on her concern. And when we landed in Scottsdale, they stayed with us— by now we had bonded, familiar faces in a new land — as we went to the baggage claim area.

The conveyor came around and Gloria, with one dainty pinky, lifted off her very slim, tiny little travel case, which looked like a diplomat's attaché case which might hold — at most — ten pieces of paper. Around came the carousel again and Scaasi and Parker lifted off their similar-sized attaché cases. They all looked at me, anxious to set off in the Town Cars waiting for us. I was hoping they would be looking elsewhere but all three were staring, in disbelief, when around came my large suitcase, which I had to man-handle off the conveyor belt with two hands. The three turned and started walking away.

"I have one more," I whispered, hoping there was not too much sweat dripping off my brow from lifting the suitcase.

A couple revolutions more and I grabbed at the large garment bag, which I pretended was as light as a feather.

Here I am with one of the perennially Best Dressed Woman of the World. Here I am with the World Famous Designer who dresses all the best dressed women of the world. And they are glancing back at me as if Bette Midler, Mariah Carey, Celine Dion, Cher — the world's biggest diva — is following them with his hourly change of attire.

Alone at last in the *Phoenician*, registered to our delight as Mr. and Mrs. Vanderbilt, giddy at finally arriving, we were like two mischievous thirteen year olds with no parental supervision. Everything was funny, everything was fun.

Truman Capote's most famous fictional creation was Holly Golightly in *Breakfast at Tiffany's*, a character he based on Gloria, his good pal in the 1940s and 1950s. There's a scene in the novel where Holly and the narrator spend a carefree day walking around the City:

> We giggled, ran, sang along the paths toward the old wooden boathouse, and then, passing a Woolworth's, she gripped my arm: "Let's steal something," she said, pulling me into the store … Holly picked up a mask and slipped it over her face; she chose another and put it on mine; then she took my hand and we walked away. It was as simple as that. Outside, we ran a few blocks, I think to make it more dramatic.

I saw during out time together in the *Phoenician* that that was vintage Gloria, and had no doubt that Gloria and Truman had done just that, and that his fictional character, Holly, captured well the Gloria he knew and I was coming to know.

The only activity that first evening was a cocktail reception and dinner in the Grand Ballroom. It was scheduled to begin at 7:00 p.m., so of course Gloria and I glamed up and found our way to be obediently there at 7:00 p.m. on the dot.

The ballroom was enormous with tables set up that easily would accommodate 1,000 guests. And not another soul in the room. It was empty.

We looked at each other.

"Do you think we could skip this?" Gloria asked me, with the answer in her pleading eyes.

We both had arisen early to be at Newark Airport for our flight. There was a two hour time difference in Arizona, so 7:00 in the Grand Ballroom was the equivalent of 9:00 p.m. at home in our pajamas. A cocktail reception, a formal dinner for over one thousand guests, a program of speakers. This evening could easily go on for four hours. One o'clock a.m. our time — way past the bedtimes of two weary travelers. Once the crowd started to fill the room, it would be harder to escape. Gloria was one of five authors being celebrated, including Scaasi and Senator John McCain. We wouldn't be missed in the mob.

"I agree. Let's escape while we can."

As quietly as two mice, we fast walked out of the Ballroom and out of the danger zone, delighted in our cunning when at last we reached the safety of our rooms.

We called Room Service, had dinner delivered, devoured it, and retired.

It wasn't long before our phones were ringing. Our doors rapped. But like Anne Frank with her family, we hid in our own attic annex.

From the moment we awoke and emerged from our rooms, we were all but put under house arrest. Two of the once lovely ladies in charge of the event were assigned to us — lovely ladies who turned into Gestapo guards — one for Gloria, one for me, her dangerous side kick, and their mission was never — never! — let us out of sight. From then on. If we had to go to the restroom, they went with us and stood right outside the door until we emerged, and walked us back to where we should be. Gloria and I looked at each other: we were trapped! This was to be our punishment for misbehaving. We looked on with envy as Scaasi wandered here and there, a free man, carefree, once coming over to us and saying under his breath, "see what happens?" wagging his finger at us as he strode away.

Somehow Scaasi at the book signing had managed to commandeer a table on a raised dais, and there he sat, looking out over his fawning subjects like a feudal lord, with Parker standing at attention behind his right shoulder, ready to protect his lord and master and carry out his wishes. I had bought several copies of his book to give to friends and stood in a line which, in its eerie orderliness, resembled nothing so much as the line making its way toward Seinfeld's Soup Nazi. When my turn had come and Scassi had honored me with his autograph — though he seemed a little put out that he had to sign three books, each with a different inscriptions to a different friend— I stepped aside and asked Parker if he would also sign them. I thought that would be a nice thing to do since he had been so gracious and so much fun and Scaasi's book, after all, had been dedicated to him, but at my modest proposal he looked instantly smitten and flustered. His impeccable patrician composure slipped, clearly he had never been asked to do this before, and he said he would have to ask is Majesty if it would be alright. I did not say what was on the tip of my tongue — "for god's sakes man, grow a pair!" — but stood aside as he got at the back of the line and patiently waited for an audience. Scassi considered this outlandish request for a moment, then rendered his verdict with an imperial wave of his hand and an exasperated "oh, alright," whereupon poor Parker signed them, with a look like he was doing something wrong, like he was defiling the Bible, and would later have to pay the inevitable penalty.

Gloria was gamely signing hundreds of books and posing for hundreds of photos. As noontime approached when she, and the other authors, would give their talk, she asked our guard if she would arrange for a taxi to be available right after lunch to take us to the airport.

Our guard sneered. "YOU are not going anywhere."

As if there had been some mistake, Gloria very politely explained that we had to be at the airport for a flight leaving at 2 o'clock.

The guard laughed, a cruel, cutting laugh. "YOU are not leaving until the afternoon reception is over."

Frightened and in horror Gloria stared at her, speechless. "But, but" she answered, "Scaasi is leaving."

Our guard, who seemed somehow to have changed out of her St. John suit into an SS uniform, complete with armband, smirked. "We don't care what Scaasi is doing. YOU will be here" and all but gave the Nazi salute.

We cringed. We cowered. Gloria called her helper in New York and after a frantic conversation whispered to me: "We're on the red eye. We'll be landing in Newark at 3:45 a.m. We have to get out of here! Today!"

And so, like the Von Trapp family singers going through their last performance in Austria before escaping over the Alps, Gloria sat down and put on her practiced smile as more guests lined up with their books and cameras.

Elated to be escaping, relieved it was over, we talked of everything on the flight home. Gloria showed me the necklace Frank Sinatra had given her which she always wore when she traveled. How she had shown it to Nancy Reagan on Air Force One when they flew with the body of the President back to California. I asked her questions about her childhood I had been curious about when writing *"Fortune's Children,"* about her recollections of The Breakers, Aunt Gertrude, her beloved nurse Dodo, whether she still had her father's horse racing trophies, details of Truman Capote's Black and White Ball. I worked up the courage to ask her how it had been to have sex with Marlon Brando when she was thirty and he had just filmed "On the Waterfront." "When you feel that way about someone" she said, "how could it be anything but wonderful?"

She told me her Scassi story — how he had seen her at a party and invited her to his atelier, where — I could picture it — like a little girl she tried on fabulous gown after gown and raved about each; how a box of them arrived by messenger the next day. Along with Scassi's invoice of close to $100,000 and how Gloria had back-pedaled out of that one by having the box returned to him along with her gracious note that it all had been a terrible mistake. She had avoided him ever since then.

Arriving in Newark the next morning to a deserted terminal, grungy, exhausted, we found our drivers and said goodbye.

My phone rang at 7:00 a.m. It was Gloria calling to see how I had slept, to recount our adventures with the lovely Nazi guards, and to tell me about the next book she wanted to write.

There would be more in the months and years ahead, more plans, more books, more fun, much more laughter.

Gloria invited me to be her guest at a dinner party at Joyce Carol Oates' home in Princeton. As with me, Joyce was another example of Gloria's philosophy in action, that "The phone can ring and your whole life can change ... Today may even be the day you meet someone who will change your life." Gloria had been moved by a poem Joyce had published in *The New Yorker*, and wrote her a fan letter to which Joyce replied, which started an abiding friendship between the two.

I arrived way too early and drove around the neighborhood for a while, trying to keep up my courage. At last, I knocked on the door and Joyce's husband, Raymond Smith, answered. Here I was, the first one there, a stranger, holding a big bouquet of tulips, praying Gloria would arrive any minute and save me. But saving was not necessary, for Ray and Joyce were immediately welcoming and thoughtful and non-threatening and showed me around their magical home deep in the woods, the portrait of them Gloria had painted, several of Gloria's Dream Box creations displayed around the rooms. If ever there was a modern day salon it was here, in the home of these quiet unassuming friends, and at this party, and others to come, I met Edmund White and Seward Johnson, Paul Krugman, a dazzling array of Princeton professors. On the couch, talking to someone, I stared at a man crossing the room who looked so familiar; he mouthed "hi" and walked over to the bar area. "Steve Martin" my couch partner whispered. "He and Joyce share a passion for art."

Gloria and I would leave together that evening after dinner, and I would walk out with her to make sure she would find her driver in the dark. "Baboo, Baboo" she would call out in a tiny voice that no one two steps from us would hear, — "Baboo" — but he always instantly appeared.

I followed her car along the dark winding country roads out to Route 206 to make sure I would find my way home. "Wherever you're going, I'm going your way."

Thank you, Gloria. Holly. My Huckleberry friend. To be with you was to experience exactly what you had talked about in your lunch speech in Scottsdale:

> "The miracle to be reborn with each day, the miracle of each
> night to descend into the darkness of dreams and wake into
> the new day. It may be the day you fall in love with a tree,

a flower, a face you see passing by in a taxi, a change in the weather. It's the miracle of the hour as day turns into night, and you turn on the radio and unexpectedly hear a song that brings back a memory of happiness so clearly that you are right back there when it happened. It may be the smell of bread baking, or a cake of soap as you unwrap it. Today may even be the day you meet someone who will change your life …"

"APPLY IT TO THE PROBLEM, GENTLEMEN"

ONCE, WHEN ANDREW CARNEGIE WAS PLAYING GOLF with Frank Nelson Doubleday, the great industrialist turned with a question for the great publisher.

"How much money did you make in your book business last month?" Carnegie asked Doubleday.

Doubleday admitted he didn't know; publishers, he explained, had no way to determine their profits on a monthly basis.

"Do you know what I would do if I were in a business in which I couldn't tell the amount of monthly profit?" the amazed Scotsman asked. "I would get out of it."[1]

J. P. Morgan did just that at the turn of the century. He had taken over Harper's, but he dropped it like a hot potato as soon as he realized that the business principles on which his empire had been built seemed to have little relevance to publishing.

Ambling along through most of the twentieth century as a cottage industry, a refined gentleman's club, book publishing has become a multinational, twenty-six billion dollar a year industry.

Twenty-six billion dollars: That's big business indeed. And fewer and fewer publishing houses are responsible for this volume of business. Other corporations sensed the presence of profits in this slumbering giant and raided it, bringing about a fantastic transformation. The wave of mergers, consolidations and acquisitions by foreign corporations has left the publishing industry with just a handful of major houses that can grab a seat at the table and bid on the megadeals that now dominate the business.

The old line publishers — the Scribners, the Doubledays, the Knopfs— were proud of publishing books that they considered of literary value. Today, as Roger Straus, Jr., has said, "A lot of publishing houses are being run by accountants, businessmen and lawyers who have very little concern for the books. They could just as well be selling string or spaghetti."[2] For example, Peter Davis, the chief executive officer of Reed International, Britain's largest publishing company, who worked his way up through the ranks of General Foods and then England's largest supermarket chain, has applied techniques of selling groceries to selling books. And found that they work.

Is it all that bad to have books treated more like commodities than art? Maybe not. Certainly in terms of finding an audience for books — which is, after all, the purpose of publishing — it's downright good. The inefficiencies, the sluggishness, the inadequate financial controls that characterized the publishing industry are being corrected. Publishers are shortening the time between when a decision is made to take on a book and when the book hits the shelves; improving sales projections and production schedules; lowering composition costs; shipping books faster; billing faster. The result has been increased productivity and sales. Any system that helps do that is not only not all that bad; it's a godsend.

The problem is that with a sharpening focus on the bottom line, houses tend to concentrate on books they believe have a high likelihood of being commercially successful, thereby restricting the range of books that might reach market. "When I began to write," John Updike remembered, "publishers were gentlemen in tweed jackets puffing pipes. Now ... publishing houses are owned by oil companies ... and their interest is naturally in the big strike, the gusher.... I don't want to write a gusher. I want to write books that unlock the traffic jam in everybody's head."[3]

Focusing on profit also means cutting overhead, which often

means cutting staff, cutting promotion budgets, and raising the price of books, all of which can lessen the quality of books and shrink their market. Change clearly can be a two-edged sword.

It's all well and good to talk about long range financial projections and profit goals, but how can sales be projected when the books on which the sales projections are based have no yet been written; when maybe their authors have not yet even been discovered; when the public's tastes are changing from year to year, even from season to season? "If somebody asks me for a five-year plan, I can't do it," Peter Mayer, the former chief executive of Penguin Books, noted. "The books are not written yet. It would be a fraud." Yet the head of the British conglomerate that owns Penguin, as well as The Financial Times and Royal Doulton china, couldn't understand this. "Royal Doulton does it, why can't you?" Mr. Mayer was constantly asked.[4] As successful a businessman as S.I. Newhouse, Jr., once overseer of that part of the Newhouse empire which once included Random House, Alfred A. Knopf, Crown Publishing, Pantheon Books, Schocken Books, Time Books, Villard Books, Vintage Books, Clarkson N. Potter, Harmony Books, Orion Books and Ballantine/del Rey/Fawcett/Ivy Books, conceded that "this is not a high-profit business. You can't think of it on a year-to-year basis, or in terms of a traditional fiscal year. What time span is reasonable? I wish I knew. We just try to manage the business through the inconsistencies and vagaries."[5] As always, publishers need quixotic faith in what they are doing and a run of gambler's luck.

Industry inefficiencies that have festered for a long time have suddenly, with a drop in book sales, become inflamed. Hardcover sales peaked in 1994 at 513 million copies sold, and have been declining at the rate of about 5 percent a year, with no let-up in sight. "The returns problem in 1996 has proved so widespread and persistent," reported Jean Srnecz, a merchandising vice president at Baker & Taylor, one of the largest book distributors, "that they industry has had to admit there is an underlying, fundamental problem."[6] As Charles Scribner, Jr., made clear in his memoir, *In the Company of Writers*, the ability of a publishing house to innovate has become the key to its success and longevity — indeed, to its survival. "If I were advising a young publisher today, I would tell him that what seems unthinkable should be thought about."[7] How times are changing! Time and again, not so long ago, Hemingway would throw his hands up in despair about how business was conducted at Scribner's. "I would never go with any other publishing house," he wrote to Charles Scribner, "but Jesus Christ I would like to put yours in order. Sometime, Charlie, you ought to hire me at a dollar a year to put your joint on a disciplined basis."[8]

What might Hemingway have done if Scribner had taken him up on his offer today? What can publishers do to catch and keep the attention of an increasingly distracted public?

Before any progress can be made, publishers must muster the courage to do the unthinkable: to look back each season to see what went right, and wrong, with their latest crop of books.

Some of the saddest reading is to thumb through a major publisher's book catalog from a year or two ago, to review their best offerings for that particular spring or fall season. These, the books that were winnowed out from the thousands of proposals submitted to them; these, the books lovingly nourished and nurtured and brought to production; these, the books which at one time meant so much, at least to their author, and maybe to their editor. Novels and nonfiction alike. These, almost all, books that now mean nothing to anybody. Skim their enthusiastic write-ups in the catalogs, write-ups that such a short time later seem so flat and lifeless, and you have to wonder: Why did the publishers ever care about this book? Why would anyone have thought it would have done well? Why did the author even bother?

There are lessons to be learned from this Monday morning quarterbacking, painful yet important lessons for the editors and publishers who, with their authors, will take the time to stop and ask and listen, rather than just plowing ahead with the next book without learning anything from the last.

Long ago, Richard Simon, the Simon of Simon & Schuster made a habit of haunting bookstores, talking with the managers and clerks, asking for their ideas and suggestions about Simon & Schuster books and what made them sell, and giving advice to the owners on how books might be better marketed through bookstores. Frightened by flagging sales, Bantam Doubleday Dell in July of 1990 sent off sixty of its top executives to spend a few days in bookstores around the country to try to gain some insight into what sells books. The president of Bantam Doubleday Dell stated that this program, which the New York Times hailed as a bold, revolutionary experiment, would be worthwhile if it caused his executives "to think about such things as why stores decide to order certain books and not others, how they display them, whether display makes a difference and what Bantam Doubleday Dell's competitors do differently and better."[9] Revolutionary or not, the executives returned to the home office with new insights, reporting such findings as the importance of book jackets in helping to sell a book.

Like Richard Simon, publishers should make such forays into the world a regular program to stay in touch with what makes their industry hum. What might they discover?

Take, for example, the critical step of putting a price on a book. Are book buyers price sensitive? That's an easy one. Are they ever!

The publication of books slipped precipitously during the Depression, from 214,334,000 copies of new books printed in 1929, down to the 1933 total of 11,790,000, thousands of which never left the warehouse . During the roaring 1980s, the market share shifted from paperbacks to hardcovers, with mass-market paperback sales growing at a rate of 6.5 percent a year from 1982 to 1989, compared to a 12.4 percent annual increase for adult hardcovers. In the leaner

1990s, these figures again reversed themselves, with mass paperback sales rising and hardcovers falling.

The price that publishers put on a new book will have a direct and significant impact on its sales. A little too low, and publishers cut into their profit margin. A little too high, and prices reach the limits of tolerance and books don't sell. Richard Simon understood the delicate sensitivity of pricing. It was he who first experimented with setting the price of books at the odd figure like $4.95 rather than $5.00, just as consumer products were marked down so that the purchaser felt he was getting something of a bargain. This quickly became standard practice.

[When Sally Bedell Smith's book, *In All His Glory. The Life of William S. Paley: The Legendary Tycoon and His Brilliant Circle*, was published by Simon & Schuster in the fall of 1990, it had everything going for it. The reviewers loved it, it was critically acclaimed, its promotion was dazzling, and to top all of that, Mr. Paley cooperated by passing away, and his death and a review of his life was front page news. But the book never touched The List. Could it be because the book was priced at $29.95, at a time when eleven of the fifteen nonfiction best-sellers were selling for under $20? As Richard Simon knew, even a good book priced above the market of the day has an awfully tall hurdle to clear.]

Every time publishers have figured out how to lower the price of books, there has been an explosive growth in the sales of books.

Before the first Pocket (paperback) Books were published on June 19, 1939, the hardcover houses begged the company not to go ahead with this hare-brained scheme, but the books were snapped up and the paperback revolution had begun. Total sales of all paperbacks in 1939, at twenty-five cents each, were three million; sales reached 231 million by 1951 and into the billions by 1990. Let's look at the top ten best-selling books of the 1970s. *The Godfather* sold

292,765 copies in hardcover, 13,225,000 in paper; *The Exorcist* sold 205,265 in hard, 11,948,000 paper; *Jonathan Livingston Seagull*, 3,192,000 hard (remember, this thin book was an inexpensive hard-cover), 7,250,000 paper; *Love Story*, 431,976 hard, 9,778,000 paper; *Jaws*, 204,281 hard, 9,210,000 paper. Sure looks like price makes a mighty big difference in sales.

Dropping the cost of books and facilitating their distribution — paperbacks are now sold at newsstands, supermarkets, department stores, airports, drug stores, bookstores, variety stores, through over 100,000 outlets nationwide, anywhere that magazines and newspapers are sold — proved a winning formula, just as it would in two other publishing revolutions, the bookclubs and the book chains. And so it will again, for the creative publisher who figures out a new twist to this old formula.

What else might publishers and editors discover as they roamed the bookstores of their communities? That it would make sense for them to devote a certain percentage of their revenues to promote reading? Expanding the market for books, getting more people interested in reading, is the only way to force those barbarians back out through the gates.

In the early 1920s, advertising expert Earnest Elmo Calkins advocated that the publishing houses advertise not specific books, but reading in general; that they band together, make contributions to a war chest, and for several years focus their advertising on the joys of reading. "Books cannot be advertised," he said, "but reading can be."[10]

Very interesting concept. And would that not, at least in the long run, accrue to the benefit of the contributing publishers? An expanding market?

J. Richard Munro, as co-chairman and chief executive officer of Time- Warner, had stated that in "industries like mine ... a literate populace is imperative to our shareholders' success. We don't have an option but to get involved."[11] Indeed publishers don't; they should be losing sleep every night worrying about the sad state of literacy in the United States.

Why couldn't reading be made fashionable? Why shouldn't shoppers frequent bookstores as often as other stores at the mall? Why can't Calvin Klein's models grace ads about the pleasures of reading? Publishers should become actively involved in promoting reading, just as Apple went into the schools and colleges to set up programs to build a market for its personal computers, just as Texas Instruments ran ads for its calculators as "tools for learning."

Readers must be recruited and enlisted by the publishing houses. At one time, publishers, the book chains, and the American Bookseller's Association were all donating money to help launch television shows about books, from a book shopping show on cable, to shows with a round- table discussion format, to programs patterned after Entertainment Tonight. "I don't know if this will succeed in helping to sell more books" said Charles Cumello, the chairman of Waldenbooks, "but I do know we've got to try something in this industry. Even the dairy business promotes itself better than we do."[12] Publishers are recognizing the power of book clubs — small groups of friends who meet regularly to discuss the books they are reading — and are sending authors to meet with them at their private homes to talk about new books. "For the first time in publishing history," said Jane Friedman, publisher of Vintage Books, a division of Random House, "we've figured out how to reach the true book addicts. We'll use this to market new titles and backlist books, but especially hidden gems that we believe book addicts would love, if only they knew they existed."[13] Here, publishers are recognizing, is the perfect spot to trigger word- of-mouth chain reactions about a book, since these are exactly the types of people who will talk about what they have been reading. Some bookstores are even getting into the act and are hosting the book clubs at their stores, with store owners suggesting titles they think the groups might enjoy.

Publishing houses and bookstores need to work together in other ways.

Together, they must re-examine the policy of permitting bookstores to return books for full credit. In what other industry does a manufacturer offer its brand-new-this-year-hot-off-the-lines model at 40 percent off list price the very first day it is for sale? What other industry sells its products on consignment, letting the distributors return the unsold product for full credit? Gradually abolishing this fully returnable policy might not be a bad idea.

This policy of selling books on consignment was first established by young Richard Simon in the 1920s. Simon himself quickly regretted what he had done. Across his publishing house's financials for 1926 he scrawled, "Bookstore returns too high!"[14] They were 3 percent. But by then it was too late. With other houses following suit, there was no turning back, and the percentage of returns kept growing. "Gone today, here tomorrow," was Alfred A. Knopf's lament.[15] "Do you keep a copy of every book you print?" a lady asked British publisher Jonathan Cape at a London cocktail party. "Madam," he replied, "I keep thousands."[16] Today, a publisher is jubilant if its returns are 20 percent or less, with a 42 percent return being average for hardcover fiction today, a return rate of 60 percent for fiction by unknown authors, and a 40 to 50 percent return just about average for mass market titles. Twenty years ago, a return rate of 10 to 15 percent was standard.

The policy of fully returnable sales makes the retailer safe from loss. Why should he be? Why shouldn't some of the risk be on his shoulders, some of the impetus to get out and hustle books? Shouldn't it be the role of the bookstores to help pull in customers? In some sense, life is too easy for the bookstore owners; a popular book draws customers to their stores, regardless of what the store owners do or don't do. A book they have stocked that doesn't sell is no problem: All they have to do is pack it up and return it to the publisher for a refund. Isn't this sort of like heads I win, tails you lose?

Imagine what might happen if the bookstore owners got involved in helping to hustle books. Certainly the owner would be more thoughtful in evaluating what types of books his customers were interested in and would stock books accordingly, which would help publishers in setting more realistically sized printings. The owner would have an incentive to advertise to help move his books; the relatively inexpensive local ads he could run would certainly help the publisher and author in reaching readers. Richard Simon always advised the bookstore owners he visited to run ads continuously, cautioning that not all would pay off, but that the cumulative impact of establishing that bookstore as the place to buy books would well justify the expense. The bookstore owner as partner of the publisher might be more inclined to be creative in moving books, by having more author signings, by writing or sponsoring a book column for the local paper, by supplying review books for a book column, by spearheading a book segment on community cable television or the local radio station, by putting together a local best-sellers list—what is selling best in Beamer, Indiana?—by working with the schools to help introduce students to books, by dreaming up ways to capture the attention of the public, even if by no other means than those of the store owner who hired a juggler to juggle a stack of slow-selling dictionaries in his store window.

Suddenly, the store owner is a partner of author and publisher in helping to make the stock move, in helping to widen the audience for books. It can work. The feisty, literature-loving owner of the Stuart Brent Bookshop in Chicago once sold 2,400 copies of Saul Bellow's *Humboldt's Gift* when it first came out by going out of his store and stopping shoppers on the sidewalks to tell them about a wonderful new novel.

Review publications must also be enlisted into the publishers' campaign to publish well. The number of publications in which books are reviewed is abysmally low. Why is New York the only city in the nation with a Sunday book review as good as the *New York Times Book Review*? The *Boston Globe*, the leading paper of what arguably may be the most literate city in the United States, has an anemic Sunday book review section because, it says, it doesn't get enough book ads. If that's the problem, wouldn't it pay publishers to spread their advertising dollars around to other papers to help develop book review sections which should, in turn, expand the market for their books?

Every newspaper in the United States, every magazine, every journal, could have a column devoted to books that would interest their readers. Is there a hamlet so small or remote that it doesn't have at least one resident who would love the opportunity to read a book and write about it? The reviewers are happy, the publishers are happy, the authors are happy, the bookstores are happy, and perhaps the readers will be happy too, learning of books they otherwise would have known nothing about. So what if publishers wind up sending out thousands of review copies? Chances are, if those copies were shipped to bookstores, they would just be coming back to the publishers' warehouses anyway. Why not give each new book a chance to reach its full potential audience?

The handful of national publications that do review books, and whose reviews have a significant impact on the success of a book, have a serious obligation both in printing a considered review of a book and in selecting the books that will be reviewed. They have been known to waste valuable space, a *Wall Street Journal* review of Donald Trump's latest, entitled "Drivel from the Con Donald," a review in the *New Yorker* of Ronald Reagan's autobiography *An American Life*, which began: "It is hard to imagine the person who would sit down and read Ronald Reagan's newly published autobiography" — and then ran on for over eight *New Yorker* pages to tell us why.[17]

That's prime reviewing space – a column in the *Wall Street Journal*, eight pages in *The New Yorker* — all to tell the world about books the reviewers clearly felt were better forgotten.

Consider, too, this question: Why should the book review column in the daily *New York Times* devote itself to Stephen King's or John Grisham's latest, when every reader and even every non-reader already is aware of their existence and the review won't influence consumers one bit? What a waste, what a misuse, of precious space. Or guardians of the gates of which books we will or will not hear about of the 50,000 published each year: Tell us about the books we should know about.

And speaking of review copies, publishers must get over being so stingy with them.

It seems a basic proposition that the more review copies sent out, the greater the opportunities for a book receiving coverage, and hence the greater the possibilities of selling a book. And it seems a basic proposition that out of a publisher's print run of each book on its list, it expects a certain percentage of those books to be returned, to come flying back to its warehouses like homing pigeons.

Now let's mix those two propositions together. Rather than sitting around their offices waiting for the carton-loads of unsold copies to return, why don't publishers send them out as review copies when the book is first published? A publisher publishes 10,000 copies of a book; he expects to see at least (let's be conservative) 20 percent of them coming home with their tails between their legs sometime within the next twelve months. Why not send out 2,000 prepublication review copies and see if the notices, articles and reviews they garner can get the ball rolling so that not only is the run of 8,000 sold, but maybe the interest in the book will justify another printing? With a touch more investment in time and postage, those thousands of review copies could be spread across the land; and if they are sent out with just a bit of forethought on the part of the editor, author, publicist, and agent as to where and to whom they should go, both publisher and author can rest assured that a meaningful and significant effort has been made to plumb the market for the book.

Gone with the Wind was no sure hit when published. "I don't see how they expect to sell any copies," Margaret Mitchell fretted to her husband before its publication. "Don't worry about that," her husband assured her. "You and I have so many cousins, we'll sell at least five thousand copies in Georgia alone." It was the author's hope that she might earn $5,000 for her years of labor. Nor was Macmillan very sure of what it was doing. It ran a first printing of 10,000 copies and hired a publicist to help promote the book.

In setting up a book signing in a major department store in Atlanta, the publicist recommended "a small party in the book department, run a small ad in the newspaper and let her autograph her book if anyone comes."[19] Nor did the Book-of-the-Month Club have any idea that it had stumbled upon the great American novel. The judges debated the merits of the book before deciding to take it on. In June of 1936, it was the Club's book of the month, but as the head of the Club recalled, "Many subscribers, as they had a right to, chose another book."[20]

What Macmillan did, and did well, was to make a joyful noise unto the world. Margaret Mitchell's publisher sent out thousands of prepublication copies of *Gone with the Wind*, not just to the customary reviewers and critics and newspapers, but even to the smallest weeklies and periodicals across the country, and to the buyers and sales people at hundreds of bookstores. It proved to be an inexpensive and ingenious way of getting almost free publicity through the resulting reviews and mentions in the book pages. This same simple system worked equally well more recently for Scott Turow's first novel, *Presumed Innocent*, when its publisher seeded the market with a mailing of 5,000 prepublication copies. Two thousand advance copies of *The Thorn Birds* by an unknown Australian writer, Colleen McCullough, were the backbone of what *Publishers Weekly* called "the biggest publicity campaign of the year." John Naisbitt's *Megatrends* arrived on the desks of the chief executive officers of the nation's five hundred largest companies: "We created a groundswell of acknowledgement for an unknown book," commented Howard Kaminsky, then Random House's editor-in-chief.[22] A mass mailing of advance reading copies is credited with the lift-off of the 1991 best-seller *The Firm* by the then unknown John Grisham.

A current, computerized list of publications to receive review copies should be a publisher's priceless possession, continually refined and revised and updated, and always adapted to each new book, with each new book always accompanied by an appropriate covering note explaining its special relevance to the publication. With the expenditure of just a little prepublication time and effort and a little postage, a couple thousand carefully aimed review copies can open the market waiting for any book.

Should these, may these, be sent out by email? To ask the question is to answer it. For most people to read a book closely enough to review it requires reading a hard copy. The need to print out — a book! — is enough of an Everest of an obstacle to stop in their track a lot of potential reviewers.

What else might publishers be thinking when they tour their neighborhood bookstores and see the endless aisles of books? How can our books ever be found among this horde? There are today some 1.3 million books in print. Compare that overwhelming figure to the 85,000 in print in 1947. Does the world really need each of these books?

Each year approximately 50,000 new titles are published. That's a lot. If a publisher is not prepared to devote its best efforts to each book on its list, why not cut back its list? This is just what publishers have begun doing, following the lead of Phyllis Grann, when president and chief executive of the Putnam-Berkley Group, who cut her list from the 225 hardcover titles when she arrived at the scene in 1976 to about 75 by the early eighties. Macmillan trimmed its list by 25 percent between 1988 and 1991, and Simon & Schuster announced in 1989 it would cut back new titles by 10 to 15 percent.

Rather than publishing a lot of books and not devoting the necessary time and resources to each, an emerging strategy in the industry is to make certain that each book is well published, meaning that it has been capably edited and attractively printed, that the salesmen have gotten the book into the bookstores, and that there has been a well-structured marketing campaign. The result may be that a house can actually sell more books by publishing fewer books.

The major publishers have been responding to the most recent crisis of flagging sales by again trimming their lists. Simon & Schuster brought out six hundred books in 1997, fifty less than in 1996, and it was front page news when Harper Collins announced in 1997 that it was cancelling over one hundred books, even eliminating manuscripts listed in its catalog for the next season. "It's a way of trying to make sense out of the business," Anthea Disney, chief executive officer of HarperCollins, explained. "In all honesty, I don't want to publish books that we won't get behind and publish well."[23] Insiders at HarperCollins reported that they were being encouraged to focus on name authors, celebrity authors, authors who for one reason or another could attract the publicity necessary to sell huge quantities of books. Warner Books' list dropped from eighty in 1991 to sixty-nine books in 1996; ten of those books published in 1996 were best-sellers. Warner, too, is concentrating its resources on megabooks.

Might some deserving books never be published as the majors slash their lists? "I really believe a book that is really good will be published," Phyllis Grann has said, "even if it's a print run of only 4,000 or if it ends up with a small house."[24] And that's not necessarily a bad thing; that small house, may be able to devote more attention to each of its books.

Is it fiscal irrationality for publishers to attempt to bring quality books to the marketplace? The goal of publishing each book well certainly makes sense, though the understandable attempt to concentrate on the hits — a natural result of the commercialization of the industry, of corporate demands for profits, of superstore demands for big name books — may prove to be as simplistic a response to an extraordinarily difficult problem as Simon & Schuster's decision to use less expensive paper and eliminate full cloth covers. Publishing houses may be able to get a quick financial fix from the ghost- written novel of the supermodel of the month or the earnest autobiography of today's sport's hero, but for their bottom line, how much better to have published the next *The Great Gatsby*, which will sell hundreds of thousands of copies, year after year, for the next sixty years? That publishing houses believe they cannot afford the time and the risk involved in finding and nurturing the author of the next *The Great Gatsby* is the central conundrum of the new world of publishing.

Time may prove that a misplaced faith in the sales power of megabooks leads to the downfall of those houses that cling to the quick fix, and to the rise of others. The focus of the majors on big names and nonbooks opens up for some of the smaller publishers, and even for start-up houses, the opportunity to find and publish quality books. And in so doing, would it be surprising to see them rise as the next Knopf or the next Simon & Schuster?

Other publishers who have wrestled with the dilemma agree. As Charles Scribner, Jr., described it:

> The man who daily oversees the business side of publishing thinks editors are numbskulls who know nothing about money. The editors think the business manager is a yahoo who knows nothing about books. Probably every firm is

plagued in the same way. The business mind never understands that literary judgment takes imagination and flair. Even more important, the business mind never learns that best-sellers are not predictable. The truth is that business risks taken on the basis of experienced intuition alone often times pay off handsomely. That is one of the most interesting features of publishing.[25]

Maybe it's time again to mine the slush piles in search of hidden gems. Doubleday in 1974 shut down its slush pile, returning unopened the manuscripts that arrived from unknowns, and most of the major houses now will review only manuscripts submitted by an agent. Jim Landis, then an editor at William Morrow, scoffed at the notion that publishers were eliminating their slush piles because of the expense involved in reviewing each year several thousand unsolicited manuscripts when, in a typical year, only a handful would be published. "Any publisher could tell you twenty better ways to save money. The excuse I'd like to hear is that they won't read the stuff because reading it is so goddamn painful!"[26] With authors finding it more difficult to find an agent to open the door to a publishing house, and with agents focusing more of their attention on commercial books, perhaps publishers should rethink their policy on unsolicited manuscripts and have a sharp-eyed reader pan the slush pile for gold.

Another facet of having a book well published is taking advantage of today's technology to make publishing more efficient and cost effective, from the use of desk top computers to give editors the capacity to eliminate galley proofs, to centralized computer systems for accounting and inventory control–integrated computer systems which, with the touch of a key, can spit out current information on sales, inventory, and royalties. If Frito-Lay, a subsidiary of PepsiCo, can use personal computers on the desk of its thirty-two division sales managers to track what happens to each of the company's snack lines on a daily basis, enabling the company to turn on a dime from a national marketing strategy to one based on local responses, this sort of micro- marketing could be employed by publishing houses to their advantage.

Think what such a system would mean for getting books exactly to where they are needed, knowing how and where to promote a book, knowing how a book was selling, when to initiate another printing, when and where to advertise, what books to display where. Agent Mort Janklow has complained that "too many decisions in publishing are just seat-of-the-pants decisions. Colgate, for Christ's sake, won't think of introducing a new toothpaste without finding out things like 'Do people like mint?' and 'Do they like green? Or is green an offputting color?'. I go to a big book publisher and say, 'You've got millions. Do this kind of research.'"[27] Despite the industry's protestations that books are different, the technology for carrying out this type of research is available — for analyzing, for example, where the returns are coming from and how different books are selling in different types of markets, and what customers want. Suddenly the imponderables of the publishing industry are translated into facts, and the facts are known, now, and can be acted upon, now.

As publishers poke around bookstores and examine what makes their industry hum, they should carry with them a watch and a calendar. These should be required accessories for those publishers who can have such a different sense of time than their authors, those publishers who sometimes seem to have imbibed a sip or two of that strange drink the tiny Dutchmen shared with Rip Van Winkle years ago up in the Catskills. Unconscionable delays so characteristic of publishing as we know it — in responding to inquiries, in determining whether to accept or reject a manuscript, in editing it, in letting publication dates slip by, in organizing a timely promotion and publicity campaign — none of that should be a part of a multi-billion dollar industry.

Time and again, since time immemorial, publishers have laid gentle hands on their authors' anxious shoulders and said, "Patience! This all takes time." But they blew their cover when they discovered that they could publish, successfully, instant books.

Instant paperbacks to capitalize on a current news headline have been around for some time now. These books are written and published and flood the market within a matter of weeks, or days, of the news. Over 500,000 copies of *The Report of the Warren Commission* were for sale as a Bantam paperback eighty hours after the government released the document. A book on the 1967 Arab-Israeli war was written and published in twenty days. Random House had a hardcover book on Desert Storm in the bookstores within two months after the war. With the grinding recession of the early 1990s, publishers began speeding up the publication process for hardcover books, trimming the standard one year from receipt of manuscript to publication date to three or four months, to sooner achieve a return on their capital. "That old business of nine months for a nonfiction schedule has become a myth," said Ann Godoff, editor-in-chief of the Atlantic Monthly Press. "Books that are tied to a news event, books that you need to give more prominence on a list, or books that you need to get out to beat a competing title are all being published in very short deadlines." It obviously can be done. Why not keep streamlining this process? Time is money, both for the publisher and the author; the faster the publication process goes, the better for all.

Publishers, of course, don't have to tour bookstores to discover any of this — how every element in the publication of a book can be important to its sales, how nothing can be left to the inexperienced or to chance. None of these ideas of how to publish a book well are new. Every publisher has known some of them and some publishers have known a lot of them, but very few have tried consistently to apply all of them to each book they publish. It can be done. "You are in a business requiring intelligence," best-selling historian Barbara Tuchman chided her captive audience of assembled publishers; "apply it to the problem, gentlemen, solve it and don't go on and on about how nothing can be changed."[28]

There will always be that element of mystery, of magic, to what makes a book sell, but the ingredients are not a secret. They are well known. And like medieval alchemists, publishers must tend their bubbling cauldron as it fizzes and splashes, steams and sputters, tinkering with these ingredients, selecting the right manuscripts, stirring in the best title and blurbs, adding the coloring for the jacket, tossing in the author's photograph, watching the timing of when the book may best be marketed, sniffing out the right price, adding a pinch of advertising, a dash of a promotion tour, a helping of press releases, a dollop of radio, mixing and seasoning the brew to try to discover, once again, the ever-changing formula for turning an author's vision to gold.

NOTES

Send Me a Man Who Reads

1. Page, Walter H., A *Publisher's Confession*. New York: Doubleday, 1923, pp. 127-128.

2. Mortimer B. Zuckerman, "The Illiteracy Epidemic," *U.S. News & World Report,* June 12, 1989, p. 72, *The Huffington Post*, September 6, 2013; December 12, 2014.

3. John Ensor Harr, "The Crusade Against Illiteracy," *The Saturday Evening Post,* December 1988, p. 43.

4. Ann M. Morrison, "Saving Our Schools," *Fortune,* Spring 1990, p. 8.

5. *Publishers Weekly,* August 25, 1989, p. 9.

6. Christopher Hitchens, "Why We Don't Know What We Don't Know," *New York Times Magazine,* May 13, 1990, p. 32.

7. Paul Horgan, "On the Climate of Books," Wesleyan University Sesquicentennial Paper Number Three, 1981, p. 17.

8. Michener, James, *The World Is My Home*. New York: Random House, 1992, p. 278.

9. Bettmann, Otto I., *The Delights of Reading*. Boston: Godine, 1987, p. 31.

10. Charlton (ed.), p. 10.

11. Christopher Bagley, "What You Get for $500 Million in Los Angeles," *Details*, November 2015, p. 114.

12.Ib*id.,* p. 12.

13. Charlton, James and Mark, Lisbeth (eds.), *The Writer's Home Companion*. New York: Penguin, 1987, p. 117.

14. *Wall Street Journal,* August 28, 1990, p. Bl.

15. *New York Times,* June 19, 1994, p. 10.

16. Plimpton, George (ed.), *Writers at Work,* Fifth Series, New York: Penguin, p. 293.

17. *New York Times,* January 2, 1989; *Time,* May 17, 1993, p. 71.

18. Charlton (ed.), p. 13.

19. Plimpton, George (ed.), *Writers at Work.* Seventh Series, New York: Penguin, 1986, p. 121.

20. *Time,* August 6, 1990, pp. 20-21.

21. Vidal, Gore, *At Home.* New York: Random House, 1988, p. 183.

22. Moyers, Bill, *A World of Ideas.* New York: Doubleday, 1989, p. 92.

23. *The New Yorker,* May 7, 1990, p. 60

24. Hendrick Hertzber, "Roboflop," *The New Republic,* October 31, 1988, p. 18.

25. *New York Times,* January 16, 2017, p. 15.

26. *New York Times,* September 10, 1990, p. D9.

27. *Wall Street Journal,* July 7, 1993, p. Bl.

28. Dillard, Annie, *The Writing Life.* New York: Harper & Row, 1989, pp. 52-53.

29. Oates, Joyce Carol, *First Person Singular.* Princeton, New Jersey: Ontario Review, 1985, pp. 16-17.

30. David Streitfeld, "Life at Random," *New York,* August 5, 1991, p.39.

31. Bennett, Paul A., *Portrait of a Publisher.* New York: The Typophiles, 1965, Volume 1, p. 262.

32. Reprinted in Shrodes, Caroline; Josephson, Clifford; Wilson, James R. *Reading for Rhetoric,* New York: The MacMillan Company, p. 214 *et. seq.*

33. Bruni, Frank. "College, Poetry and Purpose." *The New York Times,* February 18, 2015, p. A21.

The Baffling Case of F. Scott Fitzgerald

1. *New York Times*, January 10, 1987, p. 4.

2. Newquist, Roy, *Counterpoint*, p. 410.

3. Mizener, Arthur, *The Far Side of Paradise*, p. 78.

4. Wilson, Edmund (ed.), *The Crack-Up*, p. 86.

5. Phillips, Larry (ed.), *F. Scott Fitzgerald on Writing*, p. 109.

6. Wilson (ed.), p. 85.

7. Ibid.

8. Fitzgerald, F. Scott, *Afternoon of an Author*, p. 85.

9. Turnbull, Andrew, *Scott Fitzgerald*, p. 137.

10. Fitzgerald, p. 86.

11. Ibid.

12. Turnbull, p. 139,

13. Wheelock, John Hall (ed.), *Editor to Author*, p. 17.

14. Ibid., p. 15.

15. Mizener, p. 112.

16. Wilson (ed.), p. 86.

17. Ibid., p. 88.

18. Ibid.

19. Turnbull, p. 139.

20. Fitzgerald, p. 85.

21. Ibid., p. 86.

22. Ibid.

23. Burlingame, Roger, *Of Making Many Books*, p. 3.

24. Silverman, Al, (ed.). *The Book of the Month*, p. 74.

25. *Newsweek*, June 18, 1984, p. 93.

26. Mizener, p. 128.

27. Wilson (ed.), p. 90.

28. *New York Times*, April 15, 1981.

29. *People*, September 22,1980, p. 57.

30. *New York Times Book Review*, June 22,1980, p. 8.

31. *Newsweek*, May 26,1980, p. 86.

32. *Horizon*, September 1980, p. 6.

33. *New York Times*, April 15,1981.

34. *Horizon*, June 1981, p. 9.

35. *New York Times Book Review*, June 22,1980, p. 8.

36. *Horizon*, September 1980, p. 6.

37. *New York Times*, April 15,1981, p. 14. This editor Mrs. Toole was refer-ring to was Robert Gottlieb, one of the most prominent editors of the sec-ond half of the twentieth century. In his memoirs published in 2016, Gottli-eb refers to his turning down of this book as his "most conspicuous failure." Gottlieb re-read *A Confederacy of Dunces* fifty years later as he was writing his memoirs and found that his opinion of it had not changed, demonstrat-ing once again how the right book simply may fall into the wrong hands. Gottlieb, Robert, *Avid Reader: A Life*, p. 90.

38. Turnbull, p. 115.

39. Wilson (ed.), p. 86.

40. Turnbull, Andrew, (ed.). *The Letters of F. Scott Fitzgerald*, p. 357.

41. Wheelock (ed.), p. 230.

42. Ibid., p. 385.

43. Turnbull (ed.), *The Letters of F. Scott Fitzgerald*, p. 404.

44. Wheelock (ed.), p. 405.

45. Ibid., p. 384.

46. Bruccoli, Matthew J. (ed.), *The Short Stories of F. Scott Fitzgerald*, p. ix.

47. Scribner, Charles, Jr., *In the Company of Writers*, p. 161.

48. Trollope, Anthony, *An Autobiography*, p. 14.

49. Gottlieb, p. 90.

50. Baker, Carlos (ed.), *Ernest Hemingway*, p. 119.

51. Plimpton, George (ed.). *Writers at Work*, Sixth Series, p. 84.

52. Plimpton, George (ed.). *Writers at Work*, Eighth Series, p. 307.

53. Book-of-the-Month Club "Book News" Special Issue, (October-No-vember 1991), p. 2.

54. *New York Times*, January 13,1993, p. C20.

55. Hart, James D., *The Popular Book*, p. 288.

56. Turnbull (ed.), *The Letters of F. Scott Fitzgerald*, p. 168.

57.Ibid., p. 169

58.Ibid., p. 170

59.Ibid., p. 177

60. Joanne Kaufman, "Books as Tough to Name as Babies," *The Wall Street Journal*, May 7, 1991, p. A20.

An Author In Search of a Character

1. Clarke, Gerald, *Capote – A Biography*, p. 173.

2. Vidal, Gore, *Palimpsest: A Memoir*, p. 179.

3. Ibid, pp. 25, 26.

4.Ibid., p. 82.

5.Ibid., p. 83.

6.Ibid., p. 31.

7. Mewshaw, Michael, *Sympathy for the Devil: Four Decades of Friendship with Gore Vidal*, p. 130.

8. Vidal, p. 281.

9.Ibid., p. 27.

10. Kaplan, Fred, *Gore Vidal: A Biography*, p. 785.

11. Vidal, p. 84.

12.Ibid., p. 32.

13.Ibid., p. 34.

14.Ibid., p. 312.

15.Ibid., p. 35.

16.Ibid.

17.Ibid., p. 166.

18.Ibid., 34-35.

19. Dick, Bernard, *The Apostate Angel: A Critical Study of Gore Vidal*, p. 13.

20. Vidal, *Palimpsest*, p. 174.

21. Vidal, *The Last Empire. Essays: 1991-2000*, p. 115.

22. Vidal, *At Home. Essays: 1982-1988*, p. 289.

23. Vidal, *Palimpsest*, p. 169. Surprisingly, in light of his friendship with Gore Vidal and being in Paris at the same time, there is no evidence that Tennessee Williams ever met Denham Fouts.

24. Bucknell, Katherine (editor) *Christopher Isherwood Diaries: Volume One: 1939-1960*, p. 401.

25. Ibid.

26. Vidal, *Palimpsest*, p. 176.

27. Plimpton, George (editor), *Truman Capote: In Which Various Friends, Enemies, Acquaintances and Detractors Recall his Turbulent Career*, p. 89.

28. Vidal, *Palimpsest*, p. 179.

29. Ibid., pp. 179, 180.

30. Ibid., p. 180.

31. Plimpton, p. 89.

32. Bucknell, p. 402.

33. Vidal, *Palimpsest*, p. 179.

34. Ibid., p. 180.

35. Bucknell, p. 402.

36. Bucknell, Katherine, *Christopher Isherwood: Lost Years: A Memoir 1945- 1951*, p. 142.

37. Ibid., p. 142.

38. Isherwood, *My Guru and His Disciple*, p. 142.

39. Plimpton, p. 88.

40. Bucknell, *Christopher Isherwood Diaries*, p. 402.

41. Plimpton, p. 89.

42. Stanton, Robert, *Views from a Window: Conversations with Gore Vidal*, p. 92.

43. Ibid., p. 93.

44. Wishart, Michael, *High Diver*, p. 60.

45. Vidal, *The Judgment of Paris*, p. 571.
46. Vidal, *Palimpsest*, p. 100.
47. Stanton, pp. 57-58.
48. Vidal, *A Thirsty Evil*, p. 101.
49. Ibid., p. 104.
50. Ibid., pp. 104-105.
51. Ibid., p. 112.
52. Vidal, *Palimpsest*, p. 155.
53. Vidal, *A Thirsty Evil*, p. 113.
54. Ibid.
55. Vidal, *The Last Empire*, p. 308.

Recent biographers have questioned the veracity of Vidal's account of the nature of his relationship with Jimmie Trimble, which, of course is unknowable without the testimony of Trimble. They cite comments such as a St. Alban's prep school friend of both Gore and Jimmie who stated: "What nonsense all of that is. I suspect none of that sexual business ever happened. Jimmie wasn't that kind of fellow. He would have hit Gore in the nose, hard. Everything in Gore's memories of Jimmie fits into the category of fantasy." (Parini, Jay, *Empire of Self: A Life of Gore Vidal*, p. 26). And they cite Vidal's half-sister who has stated that "Gore and Jimmie didn't happen . . . they didn't have sex." (Mewshew, p. 156). And they cite Jimmie's girlfriend, Christine White, offended that Vidal "outed" Jimmie fifty years after his death, who stated that "Jimmie had never once mentioned Vidal" (Mewshew, p. 156). And they cite Vidal's partner of fifty-three years, Howard Austen, who said "It was like he [Jimmie] came out of nowhere when Gore was writing *Palimpsest*." (Parini, p.26). "I don't even believe it, not so much." (Parini, p. 48).

Comments such as these, of course, are not dispositive of anything. All such speculation brings to mind Vidal's comment that "what ought not to be is not and must be blacked out." (Vidal, *At Home: Essays, 1982-1988*, p. 289).

Stacked on the other side of the equation is Vidal's life-long devotion to Jimmie, who appears again and again, in different guises, in Vidal's writings throughout his life, from *The City and the Pillar* (1948), *The Season of Comfort* (1949), *The Judgment of Paris* (1952), *A Thirsty Evil* (1956), *Wash-*

ington, D.C. (1967), *Two Sisters* (1970), *The Smithsonian Institution* (1998), and through his memoir *Palimpsest* (1995); the life-size portrait of Jimmie which always hung in his bedroom; his selection of a burial plot in Rock Creek Park Cemetery in Washington, D.C., as close to Jimmie's as possible.

Whatever the reality of their relationship, Jimmie Trimble clearly had a significant impact on Gore Vidal's adult life.

A thorough review of the Jimmie Trimble story appears in *In Bed With Gore Vidal* by Tim Teeman (2013).

A Character In Search Of An Author

1. Pryce-Jones, *The Bonus of Laughter*, p. 31.

2. Pryce-Jones, *Cyril Connolly*, p. 136.

3. Murray, Aldous Huxley, p. 91.

4. Bell, *The Diary of Virginia Woolf*, pp. 78-79.

5. Pryce-Jones, *The Bonus of Laughter*, p. 31.

6. *Ibid.*

7. Graves and Hodge, *The Long Weekend*, p. 114.

8. Lancaster, *Brian Howard*, p. 101.

9. Murray, pp. 100-101.

10. Benkovitz, *Ronald Firbank*, p. 125.

11. *Ibid.*, p. 181.

12. Taylor, *Bright Young People*, p. 286.

13. Benkovitz, p. 110.

14. *Ibid.*, p. 112.

15. *Ibid.*, p. 189.

16. Taylor, p. 232.

17. Benkovitz, p. 182.

18. *Ibid.*

19. *Ibid.*, p. 189.

20. Pryce-Jones, *The Bonus of Laughter*

21. *Ibid.*, p. 31.

22. Taylor, p. 232.

23. Benkovitz, p. 249.

24. Plimpton, *Truman Capote*, p. 88.

25. Murray, p. 166.

26. Pryce-Jones, *The Bonus of Laughter*, p. 33.

27. *Ibid.*, p. 31.

28. Pryce-Jones, *The Bonus of Laughter*, p. 33.

29. Ibid., p. 31. Plimpton, p. 87.

30. Pryce-Jones, *The Bonus of Laughter*, p. 31.

31. Montgomery-Massingberd, *Great Houses of England and Wales*, p. 209

32. Kaczynski, *Perdurabo*, p. 435.

33. Montgomery-Massingberd, p. 212.

34. Wishart, *High Diver*, p. 52.

35. Plimpton, pp. 87-88.

36. Hibbard, *Paul Bowles Magic & Morocco*, p. 68.

37. Symonds, *The Beast 666*, pp. 566-567.

38. Unpublished Diaries of Aleister Crowley, p. 20.

39..Bevan, "The Spying Welsh Lord, His Occult Secrets, and the Dancing Kangaroo," April 29, 2013, Wales Online.

De Gustibus Non Est Disputandum

1. Updike, John, *Picked-Up Pieces*, pp. 397, 398, 402.

2. Theroux, Paul, *Sunrise with Seamonsters*, p. 5.

3. Roberts, Kenneth, *I Wanted to Write*, p. 347.

4. Boyd, Brian, "The Year of 'Lolita,'" *New York Times Book Review*, September 8, 1991, p.1.

5. Atwan, Robert; Orton, Barry, and Vesterman, William, *American Mass Media*, p. 132.

6. Henderson, Bill (ed.), *Rotten Reviews*, p. 42.

7. *Ibid.*, p. 41.

8. *Ibid.*, p. 47.

9. Henderson, Bill (ed.), *Rotten Reviews II*, p. 29.

10. Bennett, Arnold (ed.), *Portrait of a Publisher*, Volume I, p. 250.

11. Henderson, Bill (ed.), *The Art of Literary Publishing*, p. 241.

12. Plimpton, George (ed.), *Writers at Work*, Seventh Series, p. 16.

13. *New York Times Book Review*, October 27, 1991, p. 21.

14. *Wall Street Journal*, November 11, 1991, p. B1.

15. *New York Times Book Review*, July 9, 1989, p. 15.

16. *Time*, November 20, 1989.

17. Kingston, Paul, *The Wages of Writing*, p. 86.

18. Cheever, John, *The Letters of John Cheever*, p. 268.

19. Vidal, Gore, *At Home*, p. 288.

20. Ruas, Charles, *Conversations with American Writers*, p. 64.

21. Vidal, p. 289.

22. *Ibid.*, p. 45.

23. Winokur, Jon (ed.), *Writers on Writings*, p. 120.

24. *Ibid.*, p. 124.

25. Plimpton, George (ed.), *Writers at Work*, Second Series, p. 304.

26. Sarton, May, *Recovering*, p. 21.

27. Winokur (ed.), p. 114.

28. Cheever, p. 277.

29. *Ibid.*, p. 197.

30. Plimpton, George (ed.), *Writers at Work*, Sixth Series, pp. 225-226.

31. Wheelock, John (ed.), *Editor to Author*, p. 69.

32. Baker, Carlos (ed.), *Ernest Hemingway*, p. 394.

33. Henderson, Bill, *Rotten Reviews II*, p. 12.

34. *New York Times Book Review*, November 17, 1991, p. 38.

35. Plimpton, George (ed.), *Writers at Work*, Third Series, p. 178.

36. Henderson, Bill (ed.), *Rotten Reviews*, p. 92.

37. *Entertainment Weekly*, April 1, 1994, p. 20; Cousins, Norman (ed.),

Writing for Love or Money, p. 106.

38. Winokur (ed.), *Writers on Writing*, p. 118.

39. Charlton, James (ed.), *The Writer's Quotation Book*, p. 89.

40. Henderson (ed.), *Rotten Reviews*, p. 71.

41. Updike, *Picked-Up Pieces*, p. 165.

42. Updike, John, *Self-Consciousness*, p. 109.

43. Cowley, Malcolm (ed.), *Writers at Work*, p. 293.

44. Grobel, Lawrence, *Conversations with Capote*, p. 160.

45. Epstein, Joseph *Plausible Prejudices*, p. 390.

46. Ruas, Charles *Conversations with American Writers*, p. 126.

47. Steinbeck, John, *Journal of a Novel*, p. 157.

48. DeMott, Robert *John Steinbeck Working Days*, p. 90.

49. Plimpton, George (ed.), *Writers at Work*, Fifth Series, p. 207.

50. Bettman, Otto, *The Delights of Reading*, p. 76.

51. Charlton, James and Mark, Lizabeth (eds.), *The Writer's Home Companion*, p. 120.

52. Plimpton, George (ed.), *Writers at Work*, Sixth Series, p. 25.

53. Ruas, p. 70.

54. Plimpton, George (ed.), *Writers at Work*, Second Series, p. 150.

55. *New York Times*, March 6, 1996, p. C4; Updike, *Picked-Up Pieces*, p. 15.

56. Cousins, Norman (ed.), *Writing for Love or Money*, p. 217.

57. Updike, *Picked-Up Pieces*, p. 15.

58. Henderson (ed.), *Rotten Reviews*, p. 91.

59. *New York Times Book Review*, May 7, 1989.

60. Plimpton, George (ed.), *Writers at Work*, Eighth Series, p. 420.

61. *New York Times Book Review*, November 22, 1992, p. 3.

62. *New York Times*, August 6, 1990, p. A13.

63. Winokur (ed.), p. 36.

Jacqueline Sussan

1. Clarke, Gerald, *Capote*, p. 415.

2. Seadman, Barbara, *Lovely Me*, p. 391.

3. Mansfield, Irving, *Life with Jackie*, p. 129.

4. Madison, Charles A., *Book Publishing in America*, p. 544.

5. Goodman, "The Truth About the Best-Seller List," *McCalls*, November 1966, p. 172.

6. Mansfield, p. 131.

7. *Ibid.*, p. 132.

8. Seadman, pp. 284, 285, 286.

9. Ken W. Purdy, "Valley of the Dollars," *Saturday Evening Post*, February 24, 1968, p. 76.

10. Petersen, Clarence, *The Bantam Story*, p. 79.

11. *New York Times Book Review*, April 1, 1973.

12. *Newsweek*, February 5, 1968.

13. Purdy, p. 78.

14. Seadman, p. 429.

15. *Ibid.*

16. Whiteside, Thomas, *The Blockbuster Complex*, pp. 25-26.

17. *Ibid.*, p. 35.

18. *Time*, June 20, 1969.

19. Seadman, p. 382.

20. Petersen, p. 80.

21. Sara Davidson, "Jacqueline Susann: The Writing Machine," *Harpers Magazine*, October 1969, p. 65.

22. *Ibid.*

23. Leonore Fleischer, "How Green Was Her Valley," *Publishers Weekly*, February 13, 1987, p. 89.

24. *Ibid.*

25. Mansfield, p. 174.

26. *Time*, June 20, 1969, p. 38.

27. Purdy, p. 78.

28. "More Guys and Dolls," *Newsweek*, June 2, 1969, p. 98.

29. Davidson, p. 66.

30. Michael Korda, "Wasn't She Great?" *The New Yorker*, August 14, 1995, p. 67.

31. Martin Kazindori, "Jackie Susann Picks up the Marbles," *New York Times Magazine*, August 12, 1973, p. 11.

32. Whiteside, p. 158.

33. *Ibid.*, pp. 162, 163.

34. *Ibid.*, p. 34. Dillard, Annie, *The Writing Life*, p. 14.

35. Korda, p. 67.

"Apply It to the Problem, Gentlemen"

1. Charlton and Mark (eds.), *The Writer's Home Companion*, pp. 13-14.

2. Henderson (ed.), *The Art of Literary Publishing*, p. 255.

3. Bettmann, *The Delights of Reading*, p. 255.

4. *New York Times*, October 1, 1990, p. D1.

5 .*Ibid.*, p. D10.

6. *New York Times*, July 7, 1997, p. Dl.

7. Scribner, *In the Company of Writers*, p. 175.

8. Baker (ed.), *Ernest Hemingway*, pp. 705, 704.

9. *New York Times*, July 30, 1990, p. Dl.

10. Tebbel, *Between Covers*, p. 309.

11. *Publishers Weekly*, November 17, 1989, p. 10.

12. *Wall Street Journal*, July 7, 1993, p. Bl.

13. *Wall Street Journal*, March 30, 1993, p. Bl.

14. Schwed, *Turning the Pages*, p. 7.

15. Charlton (ed.), *The Writer's Quotation Book*, p. 101.

16. *Ibid.*

17. *Wall Street Journal,* September 13, 1990.

18. Farr, *Margaret Mitchell of Atlanta,* p. 96.

19. Charlton and Mark, pp. 42-43.

20. Silverman (ed.), *The Book of the Month,* p. 43.

21. *Publishers Weekly,* April 11, 1979.

22. Sandra Salmans, "Why Best Sellers Sell Best, and Other Publishing Secrets," *New York Times Book Review,* June 9, 1985, p. 3.

23. *New York Times,* June 27, 1997, p. 1.

24. *New York Times,* March 30, 1992, p. D8.

25. *New York Times Book Review,* December 9, 1990, p. 41.

26. *New York Times Book Review,* March 10, 1974, p. 37.

27. Whiteside, *The Blockbuster Complex,* p. 62.

28. Publishers Club Luncheon Menu: Candid Comments a la Tuchman, *Authors Guild Bulletin,* Winter 1985, p. 7

ABOUT THE AUTHOR

A graduate of Wesleyan University and the University of Virginia School of Law, Arthur T. Vanderbilt II is the author of many books of history, biography, memoirs and essays. His books have been selections of the Book-of-the-Month Club, Reader's Digest's "Today's Best Nonfiction," the Easton Press Series of the 100 Best Books of American History, and other book clubs, and have been serialized in newspapers and magazines, translated into foreign languages, excerpted in anthologies, and optioned for television and film. He lives in New Jersey.